Bluffer's ®

GUIDE TO

RUGBY

© Haynes Publishing 2018
Published October 2018

A CIP Catalogue record for this book
is available from the British Library.

ISBN: 978 1 78521 568 1 (print)
        978 1 78521 610 7 (eBook)

Library of Congress control no. 2018950620

Published by Haynes Publishing,
Sparkford, Yeovil, Somerset BA22 7JJ
Tel: 01963 440635
Int. tel: +44 1963 440635
Website: www.haynes.com

Printed in Malaysia.

Bluffer's Guide®, Bluffer's® and Bluff Your Way®
are registered trademarks.

Series Editor: David Allsop.
Front cover illustration by Alan Capel.

CONTENTS

There is a place on the pitch for everyone, including the socially inept who, as it happens, make absolutely marvellous referees.

KICKING OFF

For very nearly 200 years, rugby football has been played all around the world, and for most of those years very few people have had the faintest idea what has been going on. Beneath the heaps of bodies piled over the ball, little is seen and even less is known, but much is discussed. Rugby is a game full of bluffers.

So, even if you have never once picked up a ball and run with it, you will find in this slim volume all that you need to know, or rather all you need to appear to know, in order to enjoy the oval ball game. You will discover how the game was invented on the playing fields of an English public school, or so some people would like you to think. You might find yourself with an overwhelming urge to go and train but, with the help of this guide, you will soon realise that this is far from obligatory. You will even be provided with a selection of instant opinions that will get you through any discussion about the international professional game.

Rugby is a game rife with complex rules, regulations and some extraordinary traditions. Fortunately, very few of them need to be fully understood in order to be enjoyed. With this guide you will soon appreciate the ones that are worth knowing and the ones that are much better ignored.

It turns out that the game of rugby is essentially a warm and welcoming family, albeit one that is mildly dysfunctional and has a massive drink problem. There is a place on the pitch for everyone, including the socially inept who, as it happens, make absolutely marvellous referees. The short, the tall, the broad and the small will all find a role to play in a game that celebrates diversity and ineptitude almost as much as athletic prowess.

The game of rugby is essentially a warm and welcoming family, albeit one that is mildly dysfunctional and has a massive drink problem.

The original home of bar-room bluster and banter, rugby clubs are a bluffer's paradise. If you can hold your own, hold your nerve and hold your drink, there is a vast amount of joy, entertainment and good company to be had. You might even get a little bit of exercise into the bargain. But the moment will eventually arrive when you find yourself on the spot, which is where this short but definitive guide can offer invaluable help. It sets out to conduct you through the main danger zones encountered in discussions about rugby, and to equip you with a vocabulary and evasive technique that will minimise the risk of being rumbled as a bluffer. It will give you a few easy-to-learn hints and techniques that might even allow you to be accepted as a rugby expert of rare ability and experience – even natural sporting talent. But it will do more. It will give you the tools to impress legions of marvelling listeners with your knowledge and insight – without anyone discovering that, until you read it, you probably didn't know the difference between a hooker and a *haka*.

In the northern industrial towns, rugby became almost as popular as whippet racing, pigeon fancying and modelling for Lowry paintings.

THE HISTORY BOYS

To bluff your way through the early history of rugby, you really only need to remember one name. It's a double-barrelled name, and that of course tells you everything else you need to know.

William Webb Ellis is the name. The double-barrelling tells you that he was a public schoolboy. Fortunately, it won't be hard to remember the name of the school, because conveniently the game itself was named after it. Rugby Football was supposedly invented on the playing fields of Rugby School and, to keep things nice and simple, the school was in a town also called Rugby.

According to a plaque at the school, it was 1823 when William Webb Ellis, 'with a fine disregard for the rules of football, as played in his time, first took the ball in his arms and ran with it', and thus the game of rugby was born. It might be noted here that this was the first recorded example of cheating at football (but certainly not the last).

FOUNDER OR BOUNDER?

Webb Ellis gets a rugby ball manufacturer named after him as well as the World Cup trophy, so he certainly is a handy chap to know. Whether he truly founded the sport is somewhat up for debate. A sub-committee of Old Rugbians was formed at some point in the 1890s to consider the evidence. The records they found were conflicting and confused. He certainly existed, went to the school and subsequently became a vicar. He is buried in France and the French rugby authorities went to the trouble of restoring his grave, so the chances are he had something to do with the game. Frankly, you don't need to worry about the details. All you need to do is occasionally drop his name into conversations or match reports.

For example, 'William Webb Ellis? You played at school with him, didn't you [insert name of oldest member of your club], or was he in the year below you?' Note that this isn't a good idea if the member in question sits on the selection committee, or is a close friend of your employer.

Webb Ellis may or may not have invented the game, but his school would appear to have invented spin-doctoring. Having come up with the story, it stuck with it, etched it into a plaque and slapped its name all over the game. A trio of solicitors, who were also old boys from the school, were swiftly convened to draw up the rules, and to this day there is a museum and a lucrative little gift shop attached to the premises.

You should also know that Rugby School was where

the fictional Harry Flashman, cad, bounder, coward, liar, drunk, cheat and libertine – all the things that make an effective rugby player – bullied and blustered his way through *Tom Brown's Schooldays*. Had he actually existed, he would almost certainly have been responsible for rugby's invention. Why? Because the game came about as a result of breaking the rules, and that was Flashy's special gift.

For a spot of advanced rugby history bluffery, you need to be in the vicinity of Trafalgar Square. Tucked away behind the grand diplomatic buildings that flank Nelson and his pet lions is the site of the Pall Mall restaurant at 1 Pall Mall. Here was held the original meeting that formed the rugby union. Once again there is a plaque, so it must be true.

THE FIRST INTERNATIONAL TOUR

Rugby toddled along quite nicely from this point for a few years. Public schoolboys went up to Oxford or Cambridge and came back down again. Wherever they landed they formed a rugby club for something to do in their spare time when they weren't playing cricket or running the Empire. Chaps would challenge other chaps in other clubs to games. Tailors combined ever more garish-coloured cloth to make blazers, caps and ties.

In 1888 the first British Lions tour to Australia and New Zealand took place. You might want to point out to any cricket bluffers you encounter that the reason for the first Lions tour was a direct result of the incompetence of those organising the leather-on-willow game. For some unfathomable reason, two separate and competing British cricket-touring parties decided to head down under during the Antipodean summer of 1888. As a result, they ran into huge financial difficulties and hit upon the idea of organising a follow-up rugby tour as a way to recoup their losses.

To understand how rugby league came about, you can comfortably rely on traditional British class stereotypes to see you through.

Telegrams were dispatched and an establishment flunkie was commissioned to recruit a team of players and pop them on a boat headed for the southern hemisphere. Three of the international cricketers stayed on, while a party of 19 rugby players – mostly northerners, with a smattering of Welsh and Scottish thrown in for good measure – made the six-week journey by boat. They had a few games of rugby, winning most of them, and then reportedly played a few games of Aussie Rules football (est. 1859) and won some of those, too.

However, the key historical fact that will help the bluffer when discussing the hard-drinking antics of modern-day touring parties is that on this first Lions tour the captain, Robert Seddon, didn't make it back home at all. He drowned in a canoeing accident on the Hunter

River, having set off on his own in something called a Gladstone skiff. So when the next touring international dives off a boat into Sydney Harbour or takes a golf buggy down the M4, you can eruditely remind people of the first Lions captain who gave his life on tour, and quietly sip your pint respectfully in his memory.

THE TWO 'CODES' OF RUGBY FOOTBALL

You will also need to be sure to understand the historical circumstances surrounding the formation and early days of rugby league. For now, all you need to know is that it is another form of the game, with different rules that lead to an awful lot more running around and considerably less intimate grappling. This book focuses mainly on the version of the game known as rugby union. It is possible to enjoy both; indeed, it is possible to play both (although people tend not to). It is not possible to talk about both as if they were effectively the same game. It might be played with the same oval ball, on the same sort of pitch, with the same posts, but there the similarities end. In scoring, tackling, possession, even numbers of players, there are fundamental differences. Never be ashamed to admit to not knowing what these are. Simply say if asked (about one or the other): 'Not my code, old boy.' (Actually, don't say 'old boy' if you're north of Milton Keynes.)

To understand how rugby league came about, you can comfortably rely on traditional British class stereotypes to see you through. As rugby became popular, it was inevitable that people other than the landed gentry would take it up. In the northern industrial towns, rugby became almost as popular as whippet racing, pigeon fancying and modelling for Lowry paintings.

Down south, rugby at the time was a strictly amateur pursuit. To pay a chap for playing the game was almost as ghastly a prospect as passing the port to the right. And should a chap get a pesky injury, well, one's valet would be able to cover most of the basic errands and help administer the family estate.

However, up north some of the players had actual jobs which required the use of at least four fully functioning limbs. Pit owners didn't take kindly to players hobbling up to work with a rugby injury. Moreover, there were large crowds prepared to pay to stand around a game of rugby, and the gate money could comfortably extend to compensating players for their time spent training, playing and recovering. But the southern officials would hear none of it. 'Paying people to play would fundamentally change the nature of the game,' they harrumphed.

So a committee was convened (rugby people do like a committee) and it met in the George Hotel, Huddersfield. The *Huddersfield Examiner* of 30 August 1895 records that the committee meeting lasted for three hours; it would have been longer but fortunately no one had yet invented Powerpoint. Eventually a committee member emerged and informed the awaiting gentlemen of the press that a breakaway league had been established specifically allowing for the principle of compensating players for 'broken time'.

From this point onwards, very little of historical note

seems to have happened – at least nothing that should trouble the seasoned bluffer. The two codes of rugby ambled off merrily down their own separate paths, introducing increasingly different rules as they went along. The northerners playing rugby league, with paying crowds to entertain, ended up spending more of the game running around and being interesting to watch. The southerners playing rugby union, largely for their own amusement, ended up rolling around in a heap with their fellow players for rather more of the game.

And so it went on for 100 years with approximately nothing much terribly interesting happening until a chap called Will Carling turned up.

THE ONSET OF PROFESSIONALISM

In 1995, Will Carling was a reasonably successful England rugby union captain. He was rumoured to occasionally hang out with the young and troubled Princess Diana, popping round with a couple of replica England shirts for her boys, as you do, and possibly even instructing her in the finer points of the ruck and maul, and even the tackle. But that's enough about royal patronage of the game. With his fellow international players, Carling was beginning to tire of the complex rules surrounding expenses and sponsorship that had to be navigated around in the course of one's international rugby career. Rugby union was still officially an amateur sport, but financial arrangements were clearly being made by sides in their efforts to hold on to top-quality players. Cash was reportedly slipped into players' boots after games and pretend jobs were created which allowed them to train and play rugby full time. The secretary of the Rugby Football Union, a Mr Dudley Wood, had accused senior players of cheating – for trying to get round the rules.

Carling, however, also had one other problem. He had a chin that looked uncannily like a small child's bottom. So in a desperate attempt to ensure that he was remembered for something other than his facial features, Bumface Carling came up with the sound bite that ushered in the professional era of the game.

In the 1995 Channel 4 documentary *Fair Game*, Carling said: 'If the game is run properly as a professional game, you do not need 57 old farts running rugby.' He was referring to the committee administering rugby made up of 57 elderly gentlemen who, to this day, still run rugby and now refer to themselves, with some pride, as the 57 old farts.

Carling was promptly dismissed as England captain but equally promptly reinstated after a public outcry. The bubble had been burst, however. All the recently liberated genies steadfastly refused to go back into their former vessels of entrapment and the cats, now out of their respective bags, were running around scalded and causing all kinds of chaos. Rugby union gave up pretending to be an amateur sport and embraced its new-found professionalism.

Thus far the sky has not fallen in and the fundamental nature of the game hasn't really changed. Just as when William Webb Ellis was a lad, there are men and women all around the world enjoying the simple pleasure of picking up a ball and running with it. Some of them get paid for it; others are rewarded with camaraderie, social status and cauliflower ears.

With these few modest historical facts up your sleeve, you will appear to be far better informed than most. As you wax lyrical about the great history of the sport, you will soon discover that talking balls can be just as much fun as picking them up and running with them.

In the event that you have a good game, score a try or are generally fairly useful, make sure that someone else gets the credit.

CLUB SELECTION

The horseracing agent Lenny Goodman once said: 'I try to keep myself in the best of company and my horses in the worst of company.' A similar principle should apply to rugby. When you are watching the game or socialising in and around the game, the bluffer will take care to arrange the best possible company. When you are playing, however, you need to be sure to arrange the worst possible opposition.

The way to guarantee the weakest opposition is to make sure that you are selected for the lowest possible side. Many rugby clubs will run two or three sides. The larger clubs will have many more. Identify the third, fourth or fifth XV (*see* 'Glossary', page 117) captain and make sure that they become your new best friend. Not only will this ensure that you'll be more likely to face opponents as unfit as you are, but you'll also be able to choose your own position.

If you are prepared to do a little more homework, then the best club for the bluffer to play for is but a few mouse clicks away. First, you will need to identify your county's own rugby union.* Hidden somewhere on its website will be a selection of leagues. Ignore the first-team leagues and also the veterans' competitions and head straight for the reserves. Once you have found them, head straight for the bottom league. There you will find a selection of clubs playing at the very lowest ability levels in your area. Pick a side in the top half – not the league leaders, though, as they will be running the risk of promotion and will spend next season being comprehensively duffed up. Next, affecting a convincing limp (which will come in useful later) hobble along and make yourself known.

MAKING FRIENDS

It will be very easy to make friends with the captain of the bottom side in your club. He or she will have few friends left for you to compete with. In their weekly struggle to find players to make up a side, they will have already exhausted all their own social networks. They may even have resorted to approaching random strangers on trains to try and recruit them as players. Offer your services to them as a player and you will have a friend for life.

---

*The organisation responsible for the administration of rugby union is referred to as a rugby union (e.g., the Surrey Rugby Union). It should probably be called a rugby union union, but that would sound a bit silly. Similarly, the leagues in which rugby league teams play should be called rugby league leagues but again, they tend not to be.

The last thing you want is to be snaffled up by the coach or captain of one of the higher sides.

Once selected for a lower side, the next trick is to stay there. In the event that you have a good game, score a try, or are generally fairly useful, make sure that someone else gets the credit. The last thing you want is to be snaffled up by the coach or captain of one of the higher sides. Keep your head down and hope that no one else notices you. It may be necessary to make up some sort of story about the Inland Revenue, the Child Support Agency or your MI5 controller in order to keep your name out of any match report that might be circulated more widely around the club.

SECRETS OF SELECTION

The main secret of selection to a rugby side is turning up. Your family and friends may be moderately impressed with the fact that your services are required every weekend by one of the finest rugby clubs in the county. They may view you in a slightly different light and wonder what rippling muscles lie underneath your ill-fitting Primark suit and tie. Let them wonder. You and your fellow rugby bluffers will know that the only muscles that are rippling are the two or three required to reply to the weekly text message from your captain asking you to confirm your availability. Reply first every time and there is a good chance you will find yourself on the team sheet regardless of how well you played last week. (Then, of course, there are the muscles required to raise and drain a glass – an essential part of rugby culture which will be addressed shortly.)

GETTING PICKED

It is, however, important to remember that appearance on a team sheet, published and distributed to all club members in the middle of a week, does not in any way guarantee that you will be playing for that side and in that position come the following Saturday afternoon. There is many a slip between the selection committee minutes and the referee blowing his or her whistle at 3pm on Saturday afternoon to start off the game.

Throughout the week in any rugby club there will be an endless round of telephone calls, emails, text messages, Facebook status updates, possibly even black-and-white smoke signals emerging from the clubhouse chimney as players, opposition teams and referees cry off, cry back on, cry off again, complain about their position in the team, and complain about the team they have been selected for. Wives, girlfriends, husbands and boyfriends will pull rank every so often and demand that their loved one puts up a shelf or traipses around IKEA for the afternoon. The club captains and coaches will be negotiating, right up until the minutes before the kick-off, about who should play for which side and in which position. You may find yourself traded up to the team above, not because of anything to do with your ability but because someone else has pulled out at the last minute.

There is nothing you can do about this horse-trading. Once you hand yourself and your Saturday afternoon over to a rugby club captain, you are a commodity to be bought or sold. Simply leave your ego at home and make sure that your mobile phone is fully charged, and that your car has a full tank of petrol and a functioning satnav. Somewhere, somehow, you will get a game of rugby, but you may not know for certain where that game will be played and who you will be playing for – even whom you are playing with – until you are issued with a team shirt and have a chance to check the colour and the number on the back.

It is far better for the coach to be slightly irritated by your absence from training, and to have doubts about your level of skill and fitness, than for you to attend training and to have those doubts confirmed.

TRAINING AND HOW TO AVOID IT

Training is the sworn enemy of the rugby bluffer. To subject your finely tuned and carefully managed body to a series of strenuous stretches and draining drills is unpleasant, inconvenient, unhealthy and, for the seasoned bluffer, completely unnecessary.

Rugby training sessions are normally squeezed into an awkward corner of the week. If you are bluffing your way through a reasonably serious job as well, it can be next to impossible to get yourself to a dark, floodlit corner of a training pitch during the winter months. The trick here, of course, is to kill two birds with one stone. Bird one: tell your boss that you have to leave on time in order to get to rugby training. He or she will be impressed with your dedication to a wholesome, self-improving, sporty pursuit and will mentally pencil you in for an accelerated promotion after the next round of appraisals.

Next, take aim at birdie number two. Tell your coach that while you really do want to get to training as often as possible, you have a really busy period at the office and you are having to work late on a terribly important project involving complex negotiations across three different time zones. He or she will immediately mark you down as a serious corporate high-flyer to be schmoozed in the wider commercial interests of the club. You will soon find yourself selected in your first choice of playing position (*see* next chapter) and lined up for a prime seat at the club annual dinner, as the club treasurer attempts to wine and dine you into a sponsorship deal. Meanwhile, you can instead disappear off home early on training evenings and do very little indeed.

However, once or twice a season, it will be helpful to show your face at a training session. The important thing here, though, is to take as much care as possible to avoid the unhealthy aspect of attending training, namely the increased risk of getting hurt as you are trampled on by a bad-tempered second-team player who is trying to get selected for the firsts.

FEIGNING INJURY

The simplest way to avoid sustaining an injury at a training session is to turn up with one already in place. The coaches, captains and selection committee chair will note your presence as you join in the gentle changing-room banter. However, when the time comes to pick up a ball and head for the training pitch, instead you should head straight for the physio room, having previously identified a muscle or two with a vague, non-specific ailment. You can then, with a bit of luck and a few well-timed strategic wincing noises, blag yourself a free massage, as your teammates batter themselves into a pulp while being shouted at by their irritable and almost certainly sexually frustrated coach.

ATTENDANCE AND AVAILABILITY

At a given point in the season, coaches in every single rugby club will start trying to link attendance at training sessions with selection for games on a Saturday afternoon. Do not under any circumstances listen to them. This desperate gambit is almost always a complete lie. Coaches and captains will normally pick their sides on the basis of the players who make themselves available first. The easiest way to guarantee selection is simply to be the first to respond to the text message or email that comes from the club enquiring about your availability.

The risk if you attend training is that coaches will have an excellent opportunity to see what you are like at playing. Your lack of genuine rugby-playing ability is far more likely to be exposed on a training pitch than during an actual game. Training consists of a selection of drills arranged in such a way that everyone can witness you failing repeatedly at tasks deemed crucial for success in the sport. The seasoned bluffer will be aware, of course, that there are plenty of strategies to avoid almost all of those activities during the course of a normal game. It is far better for the coach to be slightly irritated by your absence from training, and to have doubts about your level of skill and fitness, than for you to attend training and to have those doubts confirmed.

If you really must train, and once in a blue moon is an acceptable interval for bluffers, then here are a few tips and hints as to the things to look out for and the things to avoid.

TRAINING TIPS

The first keen beans at a training session will often be the 'backs'. These worryingly eager types don't normally get to do much in a real game of rugby and so are much more willing than normal people to burn off a few calories at training. While you are still lacing up your boots and pre-ordering your post-training pint, backs will be out on the training pitch passing the ball to each other and practising their kicking at goal. These seemingly innocent pursuits are fraught with danger and risk for the unsuspecting bluffer. Do not under any circumstances join in at this point.

Passing or kicking a rugby ball is decidedly harder than it looks, but with care it can be mostly avoided. It will not have escaped your notice that rugby is played with an odd-shaped ball (why, nobody is quite sure). This lends it some slightly unhelpful aerodynamic properties that make moving it over any great distance slightly more complicated. To pass it you need to make sure that, as you throw the ball, you are directing one of the pointy ends towards the person you want to receive it. You will also want to make sure that you pass it to the person nearest to you. If they are further away than two or three metres, then sidle over closer towards them before releasing the ball.

You might notice that more ambitious players seem to be able to make the ball spin on its long axis as they pass it. This is showing off and should certainly not be attempted for the first time in front of other people. There is some very complicated physics around why this is a good idea when sending long passes – something to do with things called 'torque' and 'angular momentum'. Rest assured that absolutely no one understands the theory behind this, so feel free to sprinkle words like 'gravity', 'air resistance', 'velocity' and 'parabolic arc' into your explanation as to why you choose not to use this particular technique. Nobody will be any the wiser.

Passing or kicking a rugby ball is decidedly harder than it looks, but with care it can be mostly avoided.

There's no denying, however, that 'spin' passes do mysteriously tend to travel further and faster than normal 'releases' and, as a result, are a lot more difficult to catch. It is perfectly reasonable for the bluffer to declare, maybe even decree, that the game plan will be to keep passes short and that the side should play 'simple rugby'. 'Simple rugby' and phrases like 'getting the basics right' are an absolute godsend to the bluffer. They imply an awareness of more complex types of rugby and perhaps even a higher level of ability, while also suggesting that your teammates are not all quite up to your level and should therefore bow to your greater strategic prowess.

TOUCH TACTICS

Many a training session will start with a spot of touch rugby. This is similar to real rugby but it involves a lot more running around and should therefore be approached with caution. It is rugby without all the agreeable rest stops and can therefore be extremely tiring and trying. On the positive side, the bone-crunching tackle has been replaced with a gentle one- or two-handed tap on the hips, and as a result it is a game that can safely be enjoyed by groups of mixed sizes, ability levels and genders.

To bluff your way through touch rugby, you will need both a defensive and an offensive strategy. In the defensive game the least energy is required if you position yourself in the centre of the playing field and make yourself as wide as possible. You can then gently jog backwards as the attacking team approaches, generally blocking their progress until one of the quicker ones heads off to the far left or right of you in pursuit of glory. You can leave the futile job of running after them to one of the younger, fitter players in your side.

In attack, the strategy is completely the opposite. Here, the sensible bluffer will take a tactical position on the wing, hanging well back while the keener types run around wearing themselves out. Then, by cleverly timing your move, spotting when the momentum of the play is generally slowing down, you can have one little run, call confidently for a pass, and collect yourself a try in the corner of the pitch.

NICE TRY

'A try...what's that?' you might wonder quietly to yourself while maintaining an air of well-informed nonchalance. A try is the word given by those first rugby-playing public schoolboys for the act of placing the ball, with a modicum of downward pressure, on to the ground behind the line at your opponents' end of the pitch. In full-contact rugby union, scoring a try wins you five points. In rugby league you get four points. In touch rugby no one really bothers to keep score, but if they did you'd just get the one point.

'Why is it called a try?' you might ponder. Some say it's because scoring a try earns you the right to have a 'try' at kicking the ball at the goal for a further two points. Others believe that it is so named because it is not quite a goal but could be considered a 'nice try'. Either way, it doesn't really matter what it is called. As Shakespeare might have put it, had he been called upon to pen the Stratford-upon-Avon RFC first XV's match report, 'That which we call a rose by any other name would smell as sweet.' So as you soar gracefully over the try line with the ball in your arms, take a moment to enjoy the sweet scent of your success at having bluffed your way on to the imaginary scoreboard.

This is often a good moment to cut your losses and feign an injury. Next time you find yourself obliged to run somewhere on the pitch, wince slightly, hop on the spot two or three times, and then walk gingerly towards the water bottles, muttering about hamstrings. You can then recover and rehydrate, enjoy watching everyone else run around for a bit, and then, after a respectable interlude, retire to the bar for a well-earned pint – still limping stoically.

TACKLE BAGS

IMPORTANT: On no account whatsoever should the bluffer ever pick up a tackle bag. These are also known as pads or shields, but they're better known as bags because they resemble boxers' punch bags. In fact, they perform much the same function.

At some point during every training session, the keen coach will haul three or four large lumps of vinyl-covered foam on to the pitch. They will be spaced out at carefully chosen intervals for an exercise linked to whatever went wrong when the first team lost their last match. The bluffer should be very much on his or her guard at this point and stay as far away from the bags as possible. If necessary, stop to do up your shoelaces or jog over to the other side of the pitch to retrieve an over-kicked ball. This will buy you some time to think through your options.

Pads or bags exist to lull the unwary player into being used as cannon fodder by the first team. One group of players will brace themselves behind the bags while another will run into them as fast as they possibly can. A ball may or may not be involved, but pain and discomfort most certainly will. Clinging to a loose bit of broken webbing, the tattered bit of foam will offer you no protection whatsoever as an angry and embittered first-team back-row player takes out his frustrations on your flimsy shield.

Ideally there will be a convenient spot – somewhere not illuminated by the training pitch floodlights – where you can hide until all the bits of shredded foam have been picked up by other unsuspecting players. Then and only then is it safe to join in the exercise. Running at a tackle bag can be quite entertaining, so at this point you should fill your boots, as the saying goes. It is the closest that, as an adult, you can often get to the delights of playing on a bouncy castle. So enjoy yourself but be ready to make a speedy exit before it becomes your turn to hold one.

BAR TRAINING

With some care you may be able to partake of a little exercise, prepare your body for the prospect of playing the occasional game of rugby and, if you have taken the advice above, avoid any unnecessary injury. The club physio might, if you are lucky, organise a warm-down exercise or two. If you have managed to resist the temptation to get excessively warm in the first place, this section of the training should be relatively pleasant. Enjoy a gentle jog and a few relatively easy stretches, then make your way towards the bar. Here, the real purpose of attending training can be undertaken: signalling your availability for selection for a game at the weekend. If you are lucky and the lower team captains are desperate for players, one of them might even buy you a drink.

The unofficial job of the hooker is to complain to the referee that the ball has not been put into the middle of the scrum straight enough. Hookers can continue this aspect of their career long after their playing days are over.

KNOWING YOUR PLACE

There are many reasons why rugby is the perfect sport for the bluffer. To start with, there are 15 players on each side and each position has its own very particular tasks and techniques. This means that, although you may not know what you are supposed to be doing at any given moment in the game, there is a very strong chance that no one else on the pitch at the time knows what you are supposed to be doing, either.

You will need to pick a position. Even if you never actually play in it, your bluffery on the touchline will be improved immeasurably if you pick one particular position from which to bluff. Don't worry if you get it wrong initially. You can always change it later, although you will at some point find your natural place.

Rugby generously provides a home for all shapes and sizes; it is by far and away the most diverse and inclusive of sports. You will find yourself playing with short, squat little chaps, huge hulking beasts, beanpole-thin types and everything in between. Think *Lord of the Rings* without the good-looking cast members and you'll be somewhere close.

When you present yourself as available for selection, the first question you will be asked by a captain or coach desperate to make up a full side is, 'What position do you play?' The most helpful answer is, 'Anywhere, really.' At this point the captain will suggest the one position that he or she is currently finding hardest to fill. He or she might take a quick look at your physique, but the top priority will be to shoehorn you into the current biggest gap in the side. This could be a mistake, so you should very briefly acquaint yourself with the following foolproof guide to choosing your position on the rugby pitch.

FORWARD OR BACK?

This is rugby's version of *Men are from Mars, Women are from Venus* and a decision that will determine your whole experience of the game. Backs and forwards often train separately and have an entirely different perspective on the game. There are essentially genetic distinctions between the two subspecies and your choice will have been predetermined long ago. To figure out which you are, all you need to do is to complete the following simple questionnaire:

Do you prefer
    a) lager or
    b) bitter?

Are you built for
    a) speed or
    b) comfort?

Which of the following are you more likely to use on the top of your head:
    a) max-hold hair gel or
    b) factor-50 sunscreen?

Who ate all the pies? Was it
    a) someone other than you, as you were still doing your hair when the pies were served, or
    b) you?

When small children see you on a bus do they
    a) steal your mobile phone or
    b) cry?

Do you
    a) like your personal space or
    b) occupy quite a lot of personal space?

Which way would you least like to die:
    a) by being crushed under the weight of a small elephant while inhaling fumes from a combination of Deep Heat, alcohol and last night's curry, or
    b) by having your core body temperature reduced to something slightly below that of liquid nitrogen and then being snapped in two by a tackle out of nowhere on the one and only occasion that you are given the ball?

If you answered:
    Mostly a) You are a back. Prepare for a lifetime of standing out in the cold waiting for the forwards to let you have the ball.

Mostly b) You are a forward. It is now time for you to get to know some other forwards rather more intimately than you might have previously thought healthy.

GETTING TO KNOW THE FORWARDS:

Forwards' roles are largely dictated by the position they occupy in the 'scrum'.

The scrum is a method of restarting the game when it is stopped for a perceived infringement or when the ball has gone out of play, and is where two packs of eight players from each side pack down while the ball is placed in the middle. For many forwards, the battle that then ensues is almost the entire point of the game. Both sides attempt to heel the ball back to their side of the scrum while pushing the other side backwards. It is a trial of strength and technique that is very little understood by anyone. The bluffer need not understand this, either. All that is required is that you gently stroke your chin (hopefully not bum-shaped), nod conspiratorially, whisper the words 'dark arts' and leave it at that.

2 – Hooker

The hooker is the person in the middle of the front row of the pack whose official job is to 'hook' the ball back with their heel when it appears in the middle of the scrum. Their unofficial job is to complain to the referee that the ball has not been put into the middle of the scrum straight enough, i.e., slap bang in the middle with an equal chance of both hookers having a roughly even chance of getting it.

Hookers can continue this aspect of their career long after their playing days are over and can complain about the non-straightness of the put-in at the scrum from the terraces or from the comfort of their sofa. Former professional hookers can continue to make a living by complaining from within the confines of a TV studio.

Hookers have one other job, and that is to complain when their opponents' line-out ball is not thrown in straight either.

The bluffer is permitted to make very occasional, well-timed witty references during the course of a game to the other common usage of the word hooker, but this should not be done more than three times in any given season.

1 and 3 – Props

There are two sorts of props: looseheads and tightheads. Do not be fooled into thinking that this in some way indicates the likelihood of their respective heads becoming detached from their bodies, although this sometimes threatens to happen. Props are the two people on either side of the hooker as the scrums pack down. As the two opposing front rows lock their heads together, the tighthead prop (number three) will take up the right-hand position at the front of the scrum and find that both of his or her ears are being ground into the skull of an opposing player. The loosehead prop, however, will find that his or her left ear is able to continue its happy existence, feel the gentle breeze and listen to the birds whistling in the trees, blissfully unaware of the pain being inflicted on the ears of the fellow prop on the other side.

Props are the ultimate bluffers in rugby. They have convinced absolutely everyone else that there is something terribly complicated and difficult in the job that they do in the scrum – the so-called 'dark arts'. As a result, they are generally excused all other duties around the pitch and are permitted to adopt a remarkably laid-back approach to training, warm-ups and nutritional guidance. If they are good enough to turn up changed shortly before the kick-off and amble gently from one scrum to the next, that is thought to be more than adequate.

4 and 5 – Locks, or Second Row

Former England captain and second-row legend Bill Beaumont said: 'Playing in the second row doesn't require a lot of intelligence, really. You have to be bloody crazy to play there for a start.'

Few sane individuals, faced with the rear view of the front row, would voluntarily opt to squeeze their head in between the backsides of the hooker and a prop, then put their arm up between the legs of the prop and grab hold of what they hope is a waistband. Fewer still would attempt to stay there, with the job of 'locking' the front row into position as the opposing pack attempts to force them backwards in the mud.

Not content with this humiliation, the second-row forwards are, periodically during the game, hoisted into the air by their own shorts in order to catch the ball during the 'line-out' (parallel lines of between two and seven forwards who line up to catch a ball thrown by the hooker when the ball goes into touch). Never accept the position of lock without having first negotiated a very significant rider in the form of post-match beer. You will need it.

6 and 7 – Flankers (the artists formerly known as Wing Forwards)

This is a very popular position, hanging off the side of the scrum, which enables one to make a quick escape should the whole thing collapse. However, much is expected of flankers as a result. You will be required to be first up for every tackle and to spend much of the time running with the ball, fending off people trying to haul you to the ground for a good kicking or stamping.

There are two flankers, one on either side of the scrum, so if the other one is reasonably competent, the seasoned bluffer can usually tag along behind without having to exert too much energy unnecessarily.

Number 8

This is the grandaddy of all the forwards, positioned at the back of the scrum, with the option as to whether to push or not. The number 8 gets to decide whether to give the ball to the backs or not (usually not) and generally runs the show. This is the only player who is given a number rather than a name for the position as no one risks offending them. Number 8 is a great position for the bluffer to claim. Even if you don't get to play there, you will have put down a marker for your place in the pack and other players will be a little bit more wary of you just in case.

GETTING TO KNOW THE BACKS:

9 – Scrum-half

The scrum-half is the only back who is allowed to speak to the forwards. Not only that, but the number nine is in fact expected to order them about, insult them and swear at them in spite of being around half their size. The more nimble and diminutive bluffer can enjoy this position. Once you have done with all the shouting, and the forwards have presented the ball to you on an ermine-trimmed cushion while simultaneously holding all the opposing forwards at bay, your job is then to fling the ball as quickly as possible to your fellow backs, before resuming the task of roundly abusing your pack.

10 – Fly-half

Also known as outside-half, stand-off or first five-eighth, depending on which part of the world you are from, the fly-half is supposed to orchestrate the attack and defence of a team. To bluff your way into this pivotal role you will need two key attributes: the ability to kick the ball such that it goes off in a direction of your choosing, and an easy affinity with some great hair products. Fly-halves are typically the better-looking members of the squad and can be expected to spend the most time in front of the mirror, teasing and tousling their flowing locks. For this reason, they are rarely follicly challenged. In order to maintain their good looks, they need to develop the ability to kick the ball as far away as possible so that they can avoid being tackled and can get back to their rigorous grooming schedule as quickly as possible.

In order to maintain their good looks, fly-halves need to develop the ability to kick the ball as far away as possible so that they can avoid being tackled.

---

12 and 13 – Centres

Once in a while, when the Moon and Saturn are in alignment, the fly-half might choose to pass the ball. There, waiting patiently for their opportunity to shine, are the centres, who are never as good-looking as the fly-half and have much worse hair. The inside centre is the one closest to the fly-half and probably the bigger and stronger of the two. The outside centre is the next one along the line with broadly the same attributes, only slightly lower self-esteem and usually terrible hair.

The centre positions are good places for the less-experienced bluffer to hide. You will occasionally need to look as though you are attempting to tackle an opposition player as they run past you, but other than that you shouldn't have too much to do. In the unlikely event that you get the ball, just quickly shift it along to the next chap down the line and everyone will be happy.

11 and 14 – Wingers

It is a strange quirk of rugby that the position with the least to do and therefore the most vulnerable to hypothermia in the cold winter months is given to the scrawniest and most unhealthy specimen available to the captain for selection. In theory, wingers are meant to be quick, so that if they ever get the ball they can make a dash for the try line. However, in reality they are primarily expected to be quiet, and their most onerous duty is to run off to collect the ball if it gets kicked over a fence into someone's garden. Some will opt to wear boots in luminous Day-Glo colours in order to attract attention. The sensible ones, however, will wear several layers of thermal insulation and bring a Thermos flask.

15 – Full-back

Potentially this can be a nice spot for the bluffer from which to watch the game unfold in front of you. Every now and again someone will kick the ball in your general direction, but there will normally be enough time and space for you to work out how to avoid it.

A note of caution, however: once in a while, an opposition player will break through your team's defences and there will be nothing between them and the try line except you. Tackling at this point is pretty much obligatory and everyone will be watching, so if you can't manage that, perhaps you are better off on the wing.

EIGHTY MINUTES
(MORE OR LESS)

So congratulations are due. You have successfully bluffed your way on to a team sheet and are facing your very first game. Some 80 minutes of thrills and exhilaration await you, along with possible glory and a newly enhanced social status should the ball bounce your way and you manage to catch it. With a modest amount of preparation, your rugby-bluffing career is set for a flying start.

GET THE LOOK

You will need to get some kit together but this should be as bedraggled and permanently mud-stained as possible. Nothing exposes you as a novice more than a shop-fresh pair of shorts and a pristine pair of socks in the club colours. Far better to rummage through a local charity shop or even the club lost-property collection for a mismatched pair of socks and some torn and muddy shorts.

Some under-layers might be helpful, especially if you are going into hypothermic shock out on the wing, but resist the temptation to invest in expensive protective padding. Those catalogues and websites displaying ripped bodies clad in figure-hugging Lycra are all very well for a spot of mild daydreaming but shouldn't feature on the bluffer's bank statement. It is far better to wait until you have played a few games or are heading towards veteran status. Then you can invest in some tactical neoprene armour, with its suggestion of previous episodes of bravery on the field of play and the heroic injuries incurred as a result.

Gentlemen may be wondering at this point about protecting their more intimate bits of anatomy. You will be reassured to know that the delightful relic of 1970s sportswear, the jockstrap, has now been consigned to the hazardous medical waste bin of history. A snug pair of swimming or cycling shorts should keep everything safely out of harm's way.

You will also want to invest in a mouthguard. What you do is purchase a cheap, boil-in-the-bag variety and then spend the night before the game chafing your gums as you suck a lump of luminous plastic into shape around your teeth. You will be glad that you have done this when, in the first bit of contact on the pitch, you fall over backwards, bang your head on the ground and crunch your upper and lower jaws together.

WARMING UP

Before the game starts, your captain might suggest a spot of light warming up. This is quite possibly the best opportunity for the bluffer to shine. You will be able to run around enthusiastically, catch and pass the ball with a mild flourish, stretch the odd muscle and gently awaken a few others, all without any great risk of injury or the inconvenience of opposition players getting in the way. Throw yourself into this sufficiently and you may find that you can quietly retire to the substitutes' bench before the kick-off and stay there for the following 80 minutes.

However, if you do find yourself in the starting 15, there are only a few more preliminaries to go. There may be a short huddle with a spot of motivational profanity peppering the brief lecture from the captain on any historical grudge that is held against the opposing team. Your role here is to listen politely and, when called upon to do so, squeeze the huddle together even more tightly, imaginatively shouting the word 'Squeeze!'

PLAY!

The game is started by one of the two teams' fly-halves drop-kicking the ball into the opposition half. This is one of the many reasons why as a bluffer you do not want to be a fly-half. Not only will your hair be critically scrutinised by everyone on the field, but you will also recall that rugby balls are an odd shape and therefore very likely to bounce in an unhelpful and unpredictable manner. So why, then, you might reasonably wonder, would the entire game start by asking someone to drop the ball and then, only after it has hit the ground, attempt to kick it on the bounce? This just adds an extra level of difficulty and potential humiliation.

If the opposing team kick off, no matter where you are on the pitch there is always a possibility that the ball will come somewhere near you. If it does, then make absolutely certain that you do not catch it; otherwise, following swiftly in its wake will be one of the rhino-like opposition forwards intent on breaking one or more of your ribs. Leave the job of calling for and catching the ball to the keenest and largest person on your team. There is always one and they will enjoy the prospect of an early scrap with the oncoming pack. In scientific terms the resulting impact is known as an irresistible force meeting an immovable object, and it is always entertaining to watch. It would be, frankly, rather bad manners to deny your teammates that little pleasure.

Now, if you are a forward, your job is generally to be close to the ball, pushing your fellow forwards forward if they seem to be in a bit of a bundle around the ball. If at any point you find yourself with the ball thrust into your belly, then grip it for dear life and attempt to go forward until someone stops you. With a bit of luck one of your fellow forwards will appear and attempt to collect the ball from you.

If, however, you are a back, there is a lot less to worry about. You will generally be expected to stay a little further away from the ball in case there's any risk of you touching it. Rather like Victorian children who were instructed not to speak unless spoken to, backs are not expected to go running after the ball but to wait until the forwards see fit to pass it to them – which, frankly, isn't often.

To give themselves something to do in the meantime,

and as a way of keeping warm, backs will arrange themselves in different patterns depending on which side they think has the ball at any given moment. If your side has the ball then you and your fellow backs are expected to deport yourselves in a diagonal line across the pitch, poised to run forward at great speed to catch a succession of elegantly floated backward passes.

If at any point you find yourself with the ball thrust into your belly, then grip it for dear life and attempt to go forward until someone stops you.

Of course, the ball will very rarely emerge from your forwards, because they won't trust you to keep it, and at some point the opposition pack will get hold of the ball instead. At this point you are expected to scamper forward to create a defensive line horizontally across the pitch. This in theory makes smaller gaps for the opposition backs to run through in the unlikely event that they are given the ball by their own pack. Of course, this won't happen. Your forwards win the ball back and you run backwards to your 'attacking' diagonal formation again. This has been known to go on for the length of the entire game.

However, if as a back you do find the ball hurtling in your general direction, grab it and run as fast as your legs will carry you towards the opposition try line. You never know, you might be in luck and a gap will open up for you (the opposition assuming that you can't possibly be serious about trying to score), allowing you to place the ball on the ground under the posts and collect five points for your team.

SUPPORT PLAY

These sorts of moments of glory are very rare, so you might sensibly look towards alternative strategies for try scoring success. One of these methods is euphemistically known as 'support play'.

Support play is the art of carefully conserving your energy for the bulk of the game, avoiding too much running around. Your job during the early stages is to identify the strongest and most athletic player on your team. Then, towards the end of the game, as the other players are tiring, you should endeavour to position yourself three or four yards behind the star player.

Track their movements closely, and as soon as it looks like they are about to get the ball, start running. Your aim then is to follow them for as long as possible and be the nearest person to them. With a bit of luck, they will be tackled or just run out of breath a yard or so from the try line. At which point you scream out their name as loudly as you possibly can, hold out your hands and receive from them a perfectly timed and easy-to-catch pass. All you have to then do is allow your momentum to carry you over the line for a try.

This scenario works even better if the player you are tracking has already scored a couple of tries earlier in the game. There is a little tradition in rugby that anyone who scores a hat-trick is obliged to buy a jug of beer for the rest of the team in the bar afterwards. The more intelligent player, as he or she is heading for the line and a potential third try, will be eagerly looking around for a fellow player to carry the ball over the final feet and save them a few quid into the bargain.

NOT TACKLING

There is, however, always a possibility that you will have ended up in a side with very few try-scoring opportunities. Rugby club honorary fixture secretaries have a little bit of a reputation for putting together the occasional mismatch. This is not helped by the fact that many clubs go out of their way to make it next to impossible to assess the relative strengths of their different sides. Instead of helpfully listing their sides in numerical order according to their ability – i.e., Firsts, Seconds, Thirds, etc. – there will be A squads, B squads, Extra As and Extra Bs, along with Occasionals, Wanderers and Development sides. It is often impossible to know how well matched your teams are until you emerge from the changing room to discover that your opponents have an average height of over six-and-a-half feet, an average weight of 17 stones and have been warming up for an hour.

More often than not you will find yourself watching the opposition run repeatedly through your side's feeble defences and score a selection of easy tries. As you trudge back time after time to wait under your goalposts and watch the opposition fly-half kick home yet another conversion, the bluffer will inevitably be called upon by the captain and coaching team to put in a few more tackles.

As a bluffer, however, your job is to perfect the art of Not Tackling, a far more sophisticated, technical skill resulting in considerably less discomfort. The trick is to make sure at all times that you appear to be extremely keen to get to the opposing player with the ball, while timing your run carefully to ensure that you never quite get close enough to tackle them. A deliberately futile chase of a couple of speeding opponents as they hurtle towards your try line shows commendable commitment to the cause but should not ultimately involve putting your body at risk of any injury.

For much of the game you may well find that tackling is largely unnecessary, anyway. With a bit of luck your opposition players will a) not be terribly keen themselves to get tackled should they have the ball and b) will not immediately be aware of your lack of tackling ability. So for the opening phases of the game, if you run enthusiastically with your arms spread out wide towards opposing players in possession of the ball, the chances are that they will hastily fling the ball away to an unsuspecting teammate or scuttle off sideways to get away from you. No unpleasant tackling nonsense will therefore be required and you can play on, unscathed and with your head held high.

However, sooner or later someone will run directly towards you with the ball and there will be no alternative but to try and make some token effort at slowing them down. A little light physics may be of assistance here. In any tackle, the player most likely to come off best will be the one with the most momentum. Momentum, it turns out, is a product of mass* and velocity. So if you are blessed with a fuller figure, the good news is that you won't have to run so fast. If you are, however, a weedy little winger, you will have to rely on your blistering pace rather more if you are to survive the impact.

Tackling can also get a little easier if you can get at your opponent's centre of gravity. That, of course, supposes that your opponent is prepared to stand still long enough for you to calculate where their centre of gravity might be. Sometimes, if they're particularly rotund, it will be difficult to ascertain. Ideally, though, you want to ensure that a hard bit of your anatomy – say, for example, a bony shoulder – makes contact with a soft bit of theirs, perhaps a nice, comfy beer belly. Then wrap your arms around them in a warm, loving embrace and hang on until they either fall to the ground or agree to marry you.

Once you and the tackled player are then both on the ground, there are a wide variety of rules that come into force. No matter what you do at this stage, the chances are that you will break one or more of them. Exactly which laws are enforced at this point will depend on the age, nationality and general disposition of the person who will be the focus of the next chapter: the referee.

*See *The Bluffer's Guide to the Quantum Universe*.

Most referees will be only too happy to explain their particular interpretation of the rules, as that will also give them a little rest from running around trying to keep up with the game.

THE WHISTLE-BLOWER

Jonathan Davies, the former Welsh international rugby player, got it about right when he said, 'I think you enjoy the game more if you don't know the rules. Anyway, you're on the same wavelength as the referees.'

The simplest way for the bluffer to derive the most pleasure from the game of rugby is to waste as little time as possible worrying about those pesky rules and regulations that govern it. Indeed, having a scant disregard for the rules was part of the very foundation of the sport. When our friend, young Mr Webb Ellis, first picked up the ball and ran with it, that particular technique was not generally an accepted way of playing the game at the time.

Learning the rules is, for the bluffer, a colossal waste of time. The rules tend to change at the start of every season. By the time you have got your head around them, it is time to start working on a whole new set. It is therefore far simpler not to bother in the first place.

You can also never be entirely certain which set of rules the referee is working to on any given day, and which ones he or she is most keen to enforce. Carry on playing as best suits your own particular style of play and wait to see if the referee tries to stop you. If you do find yourself giving away the odd penalty, then politely ask the referee what you might have done to offend. Most referees will be only too happy to explain their particular interpretation of the rules, as that will also give them a little rest from running around trying to keep up with the game. You should then smile, apologise and try not to do the same thing again quite so obviously for the rest of the game.

There are a few rules that do seem to have stayed fairly constant over the years. Only being allowed to pass the ball backwards is one of the key rules that everyone appears to have settled on; even the rugby league chaps seem to abide by that one. This does, of course, require you to know which way is backwards, which is sometimes harder than it sounds. Once in a while you will emerge from a ruck or a maul and may have trouble remembering your own name or the day of the week, let alone which way round the pitch is orientated. In these circumstances, if you have personal possession of the ball, the best course is to kick it – anywhere – and pretend it was tactical.

Rucks and mauls are also features of the game that tend to excite quite a lot of regulation and refereeing. These are subtly different versions of what to the untrained eye would appear to be an entirely random heap of players. Generally speaking, it's called a maul when most of the people involved are on their feet, and it seems to be called a ruck when one or more of the players is on the ground. Regardless of which version of a steaming, malodorous heap of players you find yourself buried in, your mission is broadly similar: to try to push some or all of the heap forwards in the direction of your opponents' end of the pitch while trying to manoeuvre the ball backwards towards your scrum-half. Ideally, you will achieve this without anyone seeing how you have done it, as you will probably have broken a rule somewhere in the process.

Referees and opposition players do seem to get rather aerated about anyone spotted using their hands to move the ball backwards when it is on the ground during a ruck. You should only do this when you are absolutely certain that nobody can see you, otherwise you run the risk of giving away a penalty or having your fingers pulverised by an opposition boot.

Most other rules are designed to stop particularly good players from enjoying themselves too much and dominating the game. If, for example, a keen, speedy flanker or centre has worked out which opposition player is going to get the ball and manages to get there first, the chances are the referee will blow the whistle for offside. The rules are not really written with the dedicated bluffer in mind, so, frankly, you do not need to worry about them unduly.

However, you should focus your efforts on generally making friends with the match officials. Be kind to them, give them a little smile here and there, engage them in a little light banter, perhaps offer to make them a nice cup of tea. Do not at any point question their authority or parentage. Remember that they are probably refereeing because for one reason or another they cannot play. They would quite probably rather be in your boots but are either too old, too unhealthy or they simply have not been fortunate enough to come across this book, with all its helpful tips for bluffing your way into the game.

Ingratiating yourself with the referee is one of the best ways to ensure a good result for the team. When so much of the game and what goes on in it is a mystery to players, spectators and referees alike, there is a lot of doubt of which to seek the benefit. A rattled referee who has found a reason to dislike you is far more likely to give a marginal decision to your opponents. Finally, it isn't bribery to make sure that you buy the referee a pint or two after the game; it is simply good manners. You never know when you might encounter them on a pitch somewhere in the future. Handing the ref a case of champagne at half-time, however, is probably pushing it a bit.

Some bluffers might even consider taking up the whistle themselves. Being a referee is a perfectly respectable way to enjoy the sport, and offers numerous advantages over actually playing. In most clubs you get a changing room all to yourself. Everybody calls you Sir, or Ma'am, should you prefer. You can issue additional penalties should anyone question your rulings, randomly making a side retreat by 10 yards for anything as trivial as looking at you in a slightly quizzical manner and, in spite of this, you are reasonably unlikely to get punched during the course of a game.

All you need to do to become a referee is to be in the bar when an official one fails to turn up. A frantic captain will then appear, agitated and concerned, and offering beer. Seizing the moment, all you need to do is sound vaguely interested and you will have secured a job for the afternoon and a few pints to start off the evening.

The first task you have as a referee is to check that everyone has the right sort of studs on their boots. The correct sort are nice, rounded metal ones. The wrong sort are made of rusty nails, barbed wire and broken glass. The boot-checking ritual is more about getting the players used to the idea of doing what they are told by you. Quickly you will discover that, even though you know nothing about the game, you can easily get 30 testosterone-fuelled thugs to line up neatly and meekly offer the underside of their shoes for your inspection and approval.

You will then want to introduce yourself to the front row, chiefly because these players will be your allies if the pace of the game gets a little too quick. Typically the most unfit and unhealthy members on either side, they will, at any point in the game, be content to huddle together in one place and spend a few minutes scrummaging while you get your breath back. If it is a chilly day they will also be grateful for the opportunity to warm up a little as they generously redistribute their body heat around the team.

To call a scrum you will need to spot a pass that goes forward or notice when someone drops the ball, committing the offence known as a 'knock-on'. At the lower levels of the game these are reasonably common, so you should have plenty of rest breaks should you need them.

If one side is doing significantly better than the other, then they are probably cheating. The captain of the losing side will be more than happy to let you know which rules you are failing to enforce, so after a quick but discreet chat with him you will soon be able to even things up a little.

In the olden days when the game was first played in public schools, boys managed perfectly well without referees. Any questions about the interpretation of the rules were generally sorted out between the captains. As a new referee you can broadly come to a similar arrangement with your captains. You can then have an agreeable run around, watching the game from a far better vantage point than the spectators shivering on the touchline.

You might also want to keep a note of the score with a little notebook and pencil tucked into your sock, in case anyone is interested later.

Occasionally it will be helpful to both teams if you could take on the responsibility for identifying the spot on the pitch where any rule-breaking has taken place. After you have blown your whistle, alerting everyone to the misdemeanour, keep your eye firmly on the little patch of turf where the offence happened. This is where the game will then restart. Ignore any little fights that might have broken out between the players, jog swiftly over and mark up the point with the heel of your boot. This doesn't necessarily need to be particularly accurate; you just need to make a decision and stick to it. You might also want to keep a note of the score with a little notebook and pencil tucked into your sock, in case anyone is interested later.

Once in a while during most games a small fight will break out between a couple of the forwards. Here, your job is simple. Wait a respectful distance away until the scuffle has subsided. Then call over the captains and the main perpetrators, whereupon you are required to say but one word. This is a magic word that seems to end all rugby-related scraps. The word is 'handbags' – perhaps in the context as follows: 'I'm not sure what that was all about and I don't want to know. It looked a bit like handbags to me. Now shake hands and that's an end to it.' The comparison of their furious battle with drunken girls tottering on high heels outside a nightclub, hitting each other with handbags, while shouting, 'Leave 'im! 'Ee's not werff it', normally takes the sting out of any situation.

At various points during the second half of the game, the more unfit players will ask you the following question: 'How long, sir?' This is not an enquiry about your more intimate measurements. It is simply because they are desperately unfit and need to know how much more pain and misery they will have to endure. The captain may well have promised them that they could play just 20 minutes before being replaced by a substitute, but since none have turned up they are now on the verge of collapsing in a heap. At this point, depending on your own level of exhaustion, you can pick a number between one and 40 and then gradually reduce the number each time you are asked. When you have finally had enough of being asked the question, feel free to blow your whistle and head for the bar to claim your pint. You have earned it.

THE ART OF AVOIDANCE

The accomplished bluffer will always know when to make his or her excuses and leave. There are one or two occasions around the sport of rugby when the sensible thing to do is to be somewhere else. A match between the first and second team of the same club is one such occasion.

THE FIRST XV VERSUS SECOND XV SELECTION OR TRAINING MATCH

There comes a point in the season of every club when someone suggests a game between the first and the second team. Perhaps it will come at the beginning of the season to help make selection decisions. Perhaps it will come midway through, to fill a gap in the fixture schedule. Whenever it happens you should:

a) find a wedding to be invited to or, if there isn't one that weekend, propose to someone quickly;

b) join the army reserves and get called up for a peacekeeping mission in the Middle East; or

c) get yourself arrested.

All of the aforementioned would be preferable to, and safer ways than, spending an afternoon engaging in a first-versus-second fixture. This sort of game will only have been suggested because two or more people have a seething grudge simmering and need the cover of a rugby match to allow it to come fully to the boil. The chances are that there will be several seriously aggrieved second-team players who feel that their talents are not wholly recognised. They will be looking for an opportunity to seriously injure their opposite number on the first team, thus creating a vacancy. Meanwhile, the first team will be keen to stamp (literally) their authority on any little upstart players who might want to challenge them for their place.

Any manner of other grudges can be played out in a first-team-versus-second-team game. The advantage of playing a group of strangers from another club is that most of the time there is no specific reason to dislike your opponents or to be disliked. In a match against members of your own club, there will be players who have been quietly getting on each other's nerves for years. Such a fixture is the perfect opportunity for them to explode in a series of off-the-ball incidents.

Walk away. Don't be tempted to go anywhere near this game. You have nothing to prove or gain. Switch off your phone. Switch on the TV. Perhaps watch a Quentin

Tarantino blood-fest film or a natural history documentary about lions ripping wildebeest to pieces in HD slow motion. Nothing will be quite as gory or psychologically traumatising as the match you are skilfully avoiding.

THE COMMITTEE

After a few months of successfully bluffing your way around a rugby club, someone will sidle up to you in the bar and ask you whether you might be interested in joining the committee. The very moment that you spot anyone sidling anywhere in your vicinity with these words forming on their lips, make for the nearest emergency exit with the greatest possible speed.

Committee members can often be identified by their habit of wearing brightly coloured, stripy blazers in spite of the fact that they have never been known to sing in a barbershop quartet or sell choc ices at the seaside. Their dedication to their club and sense of civic responsibility is to be admired. However, it is best admired from a distance.

Something very unfortunate seems to happen to the very best of individuals when they become members of a committee. Warm, gregarious and cheerful souls are singled out because of their agreeable nature, general good sense and administrative competence. They are duly sidled up to and, flattered to be asked, they find themselves co-opted on to the committee. Full of grand plans and good intentions, they present themselves at the allotted time for their first meeting and, sadly, dear bluffer, it is all downhill from there.

Within a few moments of the chair opening the meeting with the words, 'Are there any apologies for absence?', the new committee member realises that he or she will never ever get the next couple of hours back. The subsequent debates about membership subscriptions, the collection of match fees, missing shirts and endless recollections from older members about how things were so much better in their day – 'We used to run eight teams, you know, and if a chap's name was on the team sheet on Tuesday to play for the seventh XV on Saturday, well, he jolly well turned up and played there whether he liked it or not. And now then, where did I put my glasses? I can't read these minutes, you know…' – and so on and so on until all the life has been sucked out of the souls of everyone else in the room.

It has been said that all committees should be made up of an odd number of people so that any vote will be clear and decisive, but that three people is probably too many. Committees are nonetheless an important part of the governance of any voluntary organisation, but that shouldn't be confused with being an important part of achieving anything.

In most rugby clubs, things get done in spite of the committee rather than because of it. There will be enthusiastic and enterprising types all around the club – captains, vice-captains, bar staff, administrators. There will be former members who, if someone buys them a pint, will be more than happy to put out some flags and post protectors before a game and turn on the hot water at half-time so that there is a steaming hot bath to get into after the game. However, for every one of those worthy volunteers getting things done, there will be a committee member somewhere trying to find a way to stop them.

So, should anyone mention the c-word in your presence, it is time to make your excuses and leave.

FINES INVOLVING ALCOHOL

The accomplished bluffer will get through most games of rugby without being noticed for doing anything too embarrassing or wrong. Noteworthy errors like calling loudly for a pass and then dropping it a yard from the try line, or being sidestepped by a morbidly obese prop, are likely to earn the unsuspecting player a post-match fine in the form of a nasty alcoholic beverage to be consumed in one go and in the full glare of the entire clubhouse.

Similarly, playing too well and winning yourself the title of 'man of the match' will also earn you the delight of another post-match drink, probably to be consumed in a race against the other side's best player. You will be made to stand on a chair and listen to the chant of, 'Get it down, you Zulu warrior, Get it down, you Zulu chief, chief, chief…'

Quite what gave overweight, beer-swilling rugby-playing types the sense that they could compare themselves with the noble and brave African warriors who gave Michael Caine and his chums such a duffing up during the battle of Rorke's Drift in 1879 is not entirely clear, but the main thing is to have finished your pint before the crowd gets on to its 19th 'chief' or breaks into a chorus of:

> *Why was (s)he born so beautiful,*
> *Why was (s)he born at all,*
> *(S)he's no ****ing use to anyone,*
> *(S)he's no ****ing use at all.*

The more sadistic rugby captains will invest in a selection of shots, combining, for example, creamy liqueurs with citrus-based products (lime juice, multi-surface kitchen cleaner) to create a cement-like consistency, and will then invent a selection of spurious reasons to encourage people to drink them. Should your name be mentioned at this point, you will need to mime the act of driving a car, whether you have a driving licence or not, and hope that someone else can quickly be found to take the drink instead of you. It is also a good idea to claim that you're on a course of antibiotics and that the ingestion of so much as a whiff of alcohol will probably kill you. In extremis, combine both driving and medication excuses. And throw in an impending conversion to Mormonism for good measure.

Very rarely, on special occasions, you may notice small groups of your teammates huddling into little groups and one of them collecting financial contributions. You may also notice one of the bar staff taking down a long, glass, spring-onion-shaped object from behind the bar. Now is the time to be worried. If you haven't been asked to contribute a pound or so to the kitty, then it is very possible that you are about to be invited, or rather instructed, to down a yard of ale.

Should this happen to you, and it will at some point, you have two options. You can opt to consume the yard fully clothed, thus allowing you to spill a fair quantity, and for that to be processed by your t-shirt and trouser fibres rather than your hapless liver. (If you are quick you may also be able to secrete a few bar towels about your person for extra absorbency.) Alternatively, you can strip off and allow as much beer as you can get away with to pour outside your belly rather than inside it. There will be cries of 'Spillage!', so a token effort at drinking some of the beer will be helpful. Remember, the more you can spill now, the less your head will hurt in the morning.

What happens on tour normally also goes on Facebook, Twitter and, if you are not very careful, your criminal record.

TOURS

It is said that what happens on tour stays on tour. That is, of course, palpable nonsense. What happens on tour normally also goes on Facebook, Twitter and, if you are not very careful, your criminal record.

However, tours are an integral part of the life of any

rugby club and, as such, you will need to know how to survive and thrive on one.

First – organise the tour yourself. This is, frankly, the only way you can guarantee your own safety and sanity. Thanks to the wonders of the Internet, it is relatively easy now to track down a rugby club near a place that you have always fancied travelling to. Email the fixture secretary, agree a date and you are sorted.

Staying in control of the arrangements also means that you get the best room in whichever hotel is unfortunate enough to have your custom. You can normally swing it so that you have the room to yourself, too, rather than having to endure snoring and other bodily tunes and delicate fragrances emerging from the prop in the bed next to you.

Second – make sure that there is a packed itinerary. Nothing is more dangerous than a rugby tour party left to its own devices. The devil makes work for idle hands, and so the flankers go and order a round of Cheeky Vimtos (two shots of port and a bottle of a luminous blue alcopop) for the idle hands to lift up to the idle mouths. Before you know it, you have 14 inebriated players parading naked through a seaside resort while you try and explain to the referee that you might be a little bit delayed for kick-off.

Third – retain an independent mode of transport at all times. Do not trust the generous club benefactor who offers to fund a coach for your tour. You may never return.

INTERNATIONAL DUTY

To bluff your way with confidence around the game of rugby, you will need to appear to understand the complexities of the international game. When it comes to media attention, rugby is essentially an international sport. Without a few nuggets of tactical international knowledge at your fingertips, you may stumble badly on the path towards accomplished blufferdom.

Fortunately for you, the globalisation of rugby has been kept relatively simple. While the sport may now be played in more than 100 countries worldwide, there are only a handful that you need to worry about. You can safely count the international rugby sides that matter without having to take your shoes and socks off.

In the northern hemisphere there are six nations that you need to know about, and they play each other every year in the same tournament, helpfully called the Six Nations: England, Wales, Scotland, Ireland, France and Italy. In the southern hemisphere, there are four that count: Australia, New Zealand, South Africa and, increasingly, Argentina. They play each other in some tournaments now and then, sharpening their skills for those moments when they set out to teach the northern hemisphere teams a salutary lesson.

So, all the bluffer needs to do is equip himself or herself with an opinion or two about each of the ten sides. Even in an increasingly politically correct world it is still more or less acceptable to draw on national stereotypes as you do this.

ENGLAND

It is perfectly reasonable for any bluffer to assume that England, if everything else remained equal, should be the best nation at rugby. Not only did England invent and export the game, but it also has more clubs and players than anywhere else. In any discussion about a poor England performance, you can pause sagely, draw your breath and reveal that, according to the International Rugby Board, England has over 2 million players of the game registered at around 2,000 clubs and, therefore, speaking frankly, there is no excuse whatsoever for the dismal performance that has just been witnessed. You will need to quickly move the subject on before you are expected to rehearse the figures for other nations but, if you are pushed and can remember, the nearest rival is South Africa with just under half a million players.

The problem with England is that most of its players are only registered with their club so that they can take part in the annual ballot for international fixture tickets. They are more likely to be competing for a place in the bar behind the stands at Twickenham than a place on the pitch.

So, although England in theory has the most players available for selection, it also seems to have the least hesitation in calling up players from other countries. You can feel free to comment on the traditional English names such as New Zealand-born Mako Vunipola and Samoan-born Manu Tuilagi in the English side as the far corners of the former Empire continue to be plundered for raw rugby talent. (Though in the case of Tuilagi, Samoa was never actually a British colony. But rules are there to be broken.)

NEW ZEALAND

Traditionally top of the world rugby rankings, New Zealand are the only side known by their kit. In an early, rather unsophisticated attempt at sports psychology, an Australian assistant coach once declared: 'We are not calling them the All Blacks this week. They are New Zealand. New Zealand is a poxy island in the South Pacific.'*†

New Zealand's national sport, national pastime and national obsession is rugby. It has been said that in New Zealand, rugby is a religion whereas in England it's only a cult. The All Blacks motto is 'Subdue and Penetrate'

*Bluffers should note that it's actually two poxy islands in the South Pacific.
† Bluffers should also note, if they want to be really pedantic, that there are a further ten New Zealand islands that are populated, and hundreds more that aren't. Australians hate to be corrected about things like this.

(which sounds a bit painful) and it will probably be the case that, for any World Cup competition between now and the last knockings of the known universe, New Zealand will be the favourite to win.

In over 100 years of international rugby, the All Blacks have won 79% of all test matches played. The next closest – though still some distance away – is South Africa (65%), followed by England (58%), France (56%), Wales (54%) and Australia (53%). These statistics make the New Zealand All Blacks the greatest ever sports team in *any* sport. This fact tends to stick in the craw of their much larger neighbour, Australia.

The All Blacks like to do a traditional Maori dance called the *haka* at the beginning of all their games. This is designed to intimidate the opposition and can indeed cause problems for bluffers. If you happen to be watching the opening rituals of a game in the company of less experienced bluffers, you might choose to point out that the words of the *haka* translate roughly as: 'This is the hairy man who fetched the sun.' You should bear in mind that, occasionally, the New Zealanders have chosen a different set of words but, frankly, no one else will know if they have done so unless there is a Maori lurking in a corner of the bar. In the latter case you should stand very still and very quiet and applaud politely at the end.

WALES

The Welsh response to the All Blacks' *haka* was to introduce community singing to the international game and, to this day, when Cardiff's Millennium Stadium is packed to the gunnels with inebriated Welshmen singing *Bread of Heaven* in full voice, it's not just the sheep who are nervous.

When the game was still vaguely amateur, the traditional Welsh industries of mining and hill farming turned out fit, strong players capable of giving any international side a run for its money. Sadly, of course, those industries have now been replaced by call centres, hairdressers, nail bars and tanning salons and, as a result, the best Welsh players to emerge in recent years are more in the mould of the elaborately coiffured and distinctly orange-tinted Gavin Henson. The former partner of singer Charlotte Church played for ten years for Wales in between reality TV appearances, which will come as no surprise.

Understanding Welsh rugby is all about understanding the 1970s. It is a decade that most people would prefer to forget, with its bad hair, terrible clothes, industrial unrest and numerous crimes against British automobile design.* For the Welsh, however, it was the decade that established them as a great rugby-playing nation – when little sides like Llanelli could beat the touring All Blacks, as they famously did in 1972.

All the bluffer needs to do to pass as an expert in Welsh rugby is to draw on the work of the comedian and songster Max Boyce. Mr Boyce wrote about a factory hidden deep underground in the Welsh mountains, where they dug out the raw material from rich seams in the rock and carved it into outside-halves for Wales. It's a fun little ditty and

---

*See *The Bluffer's Guide to Cars*.

serves as an all-purpose conversational device for the bluffer. So when a Welsh player in any position is having a good game, say: 'It looks like Max Boyce's factory is turning out some new models.' Or, if things are looking grim, perhaps you might dryly suggest that there might have been a little industrial unrest at Mr Boyce's manufacturing establishment, or else they have outsourced production to the Far East.

SCOTLAND

Scotland is cold and dark. When plants are kept in cold, dark conditions they tend to grow very tall and thin and are slightly pale, in a process known as etiolation. The same effect appears to create tall, thin, blond second-row players like Scotland's Richie Gray. On the other hand Scotland also produces wee hard men like Ian 'Mighty Mouse' McLauchlan. There is little logic in Nature.

However, if it becomes absolutely necessary to talk about Scottish rugby for any length of time, you can draw on the approach taken by sports commentator and podcaster Djuro Sen, a spokesperson for the Australian national side. When challenged about whether the Wallabies had secretly filmed the Scottish side in training, Sen responded: 'Spy on Scotland? What for?'

IRELAND

To establish yourself as an expert on the Irish contribution to rugby, the trick is not saying very much at all. Anyone Irish near you, so long as they have the decency to conform to their national stereotype, will, with a little luck, do all the talking that is necessary. You can just nod, smile and quietly sip your Guinness. There will be tales of a series of players who mysteriously all seem to have a middle name that begins with O, but you needn't worry.

> 'The Irish treat you like royalty before and after the game and kick you to pieces during it.'
> *Former England international Jeff Probyn*

Indeed, the trick with bluffing around Irish rugby is in what you don't say. There is one distinctly odd feature of Irish rugby of which no one ever speaks. In a fiercely divided island, with decades of sectarian dispute, there is one international sport that unites Ireland, north and south, and that is rugby. The international side draws on players from the Republic in the south and Ulster in the north. Though traditionally played by the Protestant upper and middle classes, the team has both Protestant and Catholic players. In the wonderfully pragmatic way of the Irish, there is a gentlemen's agreement that no one mentions the political issues in the interests of being able to play rugby at the highest international level. They have quietly come to an arrangement about which song to sing before the games, settling on something inoffensive that doesn't mention any monarchs, pipes and drums, or harps. As a result, Ireland have held their own with the top nations in rugby, while this has proven a bit more tricky in other sports.

Naturally, the astute bluffer would be advised to leave the political aspects well alone and instead rely on the considered view of Jeff Probyn, the former England international, who, with remarkable insight for a founder member of the Front Row Union Club, summed it up thus: 'The Irish treat you like royalty before and after the game and kick you to pieces during it.'

SOUTH AFRICA

While the pragmatic Irish quietly keep politics out of sight in order to allow everyone to get on with their rugby, in South Africa the game has played a huge part in the politics of bringing the new, post-apartheid country together.

The late Nelson Mandela said it himself:

In the collective memory of this country rugby will always hold a place of pride for the role it played in nation building during those first years of our new democracy.

The only problem is that South Africa's new tolerance, celebration and understanding of different races and cultures in a rainbow nation does not extend as far as opposition rugby sides. A formidable force, the Springboks will always be a tough team to beat.

FRANCE

As far as rugby goes, the French can be covered with one word: unpredictable (or *imprévisible,* if you want to show off). For any given international fixture no one has any idea how well the French will play, least of all the French, so there is no need for you to have any idea, either. Simply wipe the last dribblings of garlic butter from your moustache with a serviette, take a long meaningful drag on a Gauloise, shrug your shoulders, make a noise that is mostly exhaling (but if you insist on seeing it spelt out is approximately 'beuogh'), and pour yourself another glass of red wine.

The secret to bluffing about French rugby is not to worry about the rugby at all. Simply make sure that you have a good meal before the game and arrange to meet your mistress afterwards. If you are playing in France you might want to put these the other way around, or not; really, it is entirely up to you.

AUSTRALIA

Australians take their sport very seriously, which is why it is so much fun for the rest of the world when they lose. Australians also tend to put most of their effort into the two or three weeks immediately before the kick-off, when pithy quotes and intercontinental missiles of psychological warfare are traded with real enthusiasm by coaches and commentators.

The Australians are, however, always gracious in defeat. As the former Australian coach said of the

England rugby team that beat the Wallabies with a drop goal from Jonny Wilkinson in the dying seconds of the 2003 World Cup final: 'They were outstanding. They are the best team in the world – by one minute.' Cheers, mate.

ITALY

In 2000 Italy was invited to join the Five Nations tournament. There was a little debate about what to call the tournament now that it contained a total of six nations but, after racking their collective brains, the authorities came up with the imaginative option of calling it the Six Nations. Italy have very rapidly become everyone else's second favourite team, playing with a determination and Latin passion for the game but having the decency to lose most of the time. Every now and again they beat France or Scotland, and in 2013 they beat Ireland and France in the same season, finishing fourth. In 2016 they even managed to pull off a win against South Africa, in what was for the Springboks an unlucky 13th meeting of the two sides.

ARGENTINA

The Italy of the southern hemisphere is Argentina. They were only recently allowed to join the Tri Nations tournament with Australia, New Zealand and South Africa and turned the contest into something now drearily called the Rugby Championship. They feature in the Autumn Internationals and won the play-off for third place in the World Cup in 2007, beating the hosts France, who were presumably sulking about having not made it to the final. You might be forgiven for thinking that Argentina had only one sport (other than polo) and that would be football – which, admittedly, they're rather good at. They're slightly less good at rugby, but they should not be taken lightly. Just ask any French rugby fan.

THE REST

There are, of course, a number of other nations that play rugby. Just over 100 countries are recognised and given a world ranking by the International Rugby Board, with Finland and Greece generally bumping along the bottom. Georgia and Romania tend to dominate the Rugby Europe International Championships; this is a sort of Six Nations B league with rather more than six nations and a great thick glass ceiling at the top of it preventing any more nations from being promoted.

The Pacific Islands of Samoa, Tonga and Fiji all feature in the top end of the international rankings, and all suffer from having their best players snaffled up by other nations and professional leagues. They still take their rugby very seriously, though, and periodically grab victories over the more established sides. The Samoans were introduced to the sport by the Marist Brothers, a Catholic Institute specialising in ministering to exactly the sort of neglected young people who make useful rugby players. However, Christian principles of turning the other cheek were not much in evidence when the Samoan prime minister ran into a little bother with the international authorities in

2012. Tuilaepa Sa'ilele Malielegaoi, who also happened to be chairman of the Samoa Rugby Union, suggested that in certain circumstances hitting a referee on the head with a rock might be justified.

The Samoan prime minister ran into a little bother when he suggested that in certain circumstances hitting a referee on the head with a rock might be justified.

THE BARBARIANS

Despite there being around 100 international sides available to play against, the rugby family decided to invent one more. The Barbarians are not a nation. They are an invitational side made up of international-standard players who, for one reason or another, happen to be available on a given afternoon. They give disgruntled players who can't get a game a chance to take out their frustrations on some unsuspecting international players and generally restore their gruntle count.

The Barbarians' stated aim is to play entertaining rugby and, as a result, they traditionally decline to take opportunities to kick for goal, preferring to leave more time for weaving their way through opposition defences to score spectacular tries.

In the event that you are challenged to name the best

ever try, you can assert with great confidence that it was Gareth Edwards' one for the Barbarians against the All Blacks in 1973. On this occasion, the Barbarians side contained a generous helping of Welsh players. After a nervous start in a game that the Barbarians were far from confident of winning, Phil Bennett caught a high kick a few yards from his own try line. Rather than kicking for touch and safety, he sidestepped three All Blacks and began a sequence of events involving legendary players such as J.P.R. Williams and Derek Quinnell that ended with the late BBC Commentator Cliff Morgan saying:

This is Gareth Edwards. A dramatic start. What a score! Ooh, that fellow Edwards. What can stop a man like that?...If the greatest writer of the written word would have written that story, no one would have believed it. That really was something.

Although everyone knows that the Barbarians are not a nation, the bluffer may be able to win a cheap laugh by borrowing or adapting a line attributed to an anonymous Llanelli fan. Former Welsh rugby star Clem Thomas reported in his column in the *Observer* that during a 1972 fixture against the touring Barbarians side, when things were not going well for the home side, a supporter on the Tanner Bank was heard to shout, 'Go back to Barbaria!' (Hat tip to Alun Gibbard who recalls this story in his excellent book *Who Beat the All Blacks?*, published by Y Lolfa.)

Diehard England supporters will tell you that some of the performances they've seen at Twickers would be better suited to the sewage works than 'the home of rugby'.

THEATRES OF DREAMS

Any bluffers worth their salt should know enough about the following great international stadia to demonstrate their keen knowledge of the subject when it comes up – which it will.

ENGLAND

Twickenham in west London is the headquarters of the Rugby Football Union (RFU) and as such is known to English rugby fans as HQ. Although take care not to claim any international status for this leafy London suburb. After a little squabble about the rules with some irascible Scots in 1866, the other home nations created the International Rugby Board which is now run from Dublin. Twickenham is the largest dedicated rugby union stadium in the world; seating 82,000 fans is pretty impressive, but even more so when you realise that a significant proportion of those will be former and current forwards and therefore a little wider in the seat than the average sports spectator. The stadium is built on a former market garden, purchased by RFU committee member William Williams in 1907, and so is still occasionally referred to as 'Billie Williams's cabbage patch', but is more commonly known as just 'Twickers', which sounds like a chocolate bar (but isn't). You should also know that it is less than half a mile from the enormous Mogden Sewage Treatment Works. Diehard England supporters will tell you that some of the performances they've seen at Twickers, particularly as England crashed out in the group stages of the Rugby World Cup as hosts in 2015, would be better suited to the sewage works than 'the home of rugby'.

FRANCE
Stade de France, Paris, is the next biggest rugby stadium, with a capacity of 81,338, although it was built with the 1998 football World Cup in mind – and, *quelle horreur*, the national football team still plays there. The rest of the time it is shared by the French national rugby side and (occasionally) Stade Français, one of the most successful French rugby clubs of the modern era and one of very few club sides brave enough, and testosterone-fuelled enough, to play their rugby in bright pink shirts.

WALES
Welsh Rugby used to be played at a venue called Cardiff Arms Park, but is now played at a place which occupies more or less the same plot of earth but for some reason is now called the Millennium Stadium. This might have

something to do with the Millennium Commission, the quango-cum-slush-fund that stumped up £46 million of the £121 million that it cost to build. It might also be something to do with the fact that it opened for its first international fixture in 1999 when South Africa had the good manners to lose to their Welsh hosts.

In a nation famous for its rain, the Welsh opted for one of the largest retractable roofs in the world which can play havoc with the aerodynamics for the kickers, but does keep the spectators dry and works wonders for the acoustics during the community singing.

SCOTLAND

Murrayfield in Edinburgh claims to have hosted one of the largest-ever crowds at a rugby match when 104,000 fans packed in to see Scotland beat Wales by 12 points to 10 back in 1975. However, that was in the days before all-seater stadiums and the obesity crisis. With the addition of tartan-patterned seats and some of the largest permanent video screens in the world, Scotland's national rugby stadium can now barely squeeze in more than 67,000.

However many fans are watching, there is a tradition that they maintain a respectful silence when the opposition is preparing to kick at goal. When a penalty is given there will be a burst of librarian-style shushing around the stands, in theory so as to sportingly allow the kicker to concentrate – even if he's English. At this point the more literary bluffer might like to quote the Pulitzer Prize-winning American novelist Edith Wharton who said,

'Silence may be as variously shaded as speech', while noting that the deathly hush can be more intimidating than any of the booing and whistling that might accompany other competitive sporting moments.

The Scottish goalposts themselves are somewhat revered. In the summer of 2013, the Scottish RFU held a competition among all Scottish clubs to win the steel goalposts from Murrayfield that were replaced by a more modern set designed to be easier to erect and dismantle. Clubs around the nation were invited to stake their claim to the posts in 50 words or less, and the eventual winners were the Caithness Rugby Club in Thurso.

Caithness club secretary Shona Kirk managed to secure the posts with just 45 well-chosen words, although she felt obliged to make some of them rhyme, which probably wasn't a wise decision:

Fifty years have past
But at very long last
Caithness will have its first rugby pavilion.
But raising that quarter of a million
Has left us without a pound.
So to get these posts from that hallowed ground
Would make us the happiest club around!

The *Scotsman* newspaper reported that, thanks to Shona's poetry, the 250 children who play at Caithness every week would now have the chance to copy their international idols as they take aim at the international uprights. After a less-than-successful few years on the pitch, Scottish rugby managed to gain a PR victory by literally moving the goalposts. Meanwhile, the Scottish nation scratched its collective head as Dundee's William Topaz McGonagall, widely heralded as the worst poet in the history of verse,* was briefly toppled from his lofty throne by a fellow Scot.

AUSTRALIA

While still in its full Olympic configuration, Stadium Australia also managed to squeeze in some six-figure crowds for a few fixtures around the turn of the millennium. In 2000 a record-breaking 109,874 watched Australia lose to New Zealand by 35 points to 39. Now, however, the Sydney ground has whittled its capacity down to 83,500 by removing a tier or two and moving some of the lower stands closer to the action.

Stadium Australia has the unusual ability to morph from a rectangular pitch, for rugby union, rugby league, and the occasional football match, into an oval one for playing Aussie Rules. After hosting the final and deciding test match of the 2013 Lions tour, where the home nation slumped to a 16–41 defeat and a succession of losses to the visiting All Blacks since then, the well-informed bluffer might advise the Aussies to consider leaving Stadium Australia in the oval formation rather more often.

NEW ZEALAND

New Zealand nearly had a state-of-the-art 60,000-seater stadium built on the waterfront in Auckland when it

*See *The Bluffer's Guide to Poetry.*

hosted the 2011 World Cup. Unfortunately, somebody thought it was a good idea to involve politicians, and so ultimately nothing happened and the project was shelved. The final eventually took place in Auckland's good old Eden Park, which was built over a century ago and started life as a cricket ground. It still is a cricket ground.

There is nothing you need to know about the world's other rugby stadia.

RUGBY IN ALL ITS FORMS

Just as rugby players come in all shapes and sizes, the game has grown into a multitude of different forms. You might not necessarily want to try them all out, but you should certainly be familiar with them.

WOMEN'S RUGBY

The eagle-eyed reader will have noted that, thus far, this guide has been strictly gender neutral. More experienced connoisseurs of the game have seen far too many substantial and intimidating female players of this fine sport to risk incurring their wrath. You should remember at all times when discussing the women's game – particularly when discussing it with players of the women's game – the sentiment expressed by England and Saracens flanker Maggie Alphonsi in an interview in the *Observer*: 'The "woman" bit they used to put in seems to have gone now....It's not women's rugby. It's just rugby.' The 2011 *Sunday Times* Sportswoman of the Year is known as 'Maggie the

Machine' and has a reputation for ferocious tackling. It's probably best not to argue with her.

An article in the *Liverpool Mercury* from 27 June 1881, helpfully archived by John Birch on the website *womensrugbyhistory.blogspot.co.uk*, appears to report a game of rugby, or something very close to it, played between English and Scottish women's sides in the Cattle Market Inn Athletic Grounds in Stanley, Liverpool. Amid the descriptions of their kit, which included 'knickerbockers and high-laced boots', there are reports of touchdowns, half-time orange segments and an eventual (rare) Scottish rugby victory.

However, it wasn't until 1982 that the first official international test match took place between the Netherlands and France; the French won 4–0. The 1,000th women's test match was played in July 2013 between the two sides who by this point had risen to the top of the women's game: New Zealand and England. New Zealand won that game 29–10 and went on to win the series by three games to nil. So you can safely assume that, in the women's game the New Zealand side, known as the Black Ferns, are just as dominant and feared an opponent as their male counterparts, the All Blacks.

With very little effort, the bluffer can pass as just as knowledgeable about the male and female sides of the game. At the right moment one might casually reflect on the way men's and women's rugby were given equal billing at the 2016 Olympics, when Rugby Sevens was reintroduced as an Olympic sport.

WHEELCHAIR RUGBY

In 1977 a group of quadriplegic athletes in Winnipeg, Canada, wanted to create an alternative to wheelchair basketball. They were looking for a competitive team sport that would also allow those with limited arm and hand function to participate equally. The game they devised was called murderball, owing to the rather violent collisions between chair, floor and human flesh and bone that it encouraged. After a little while, and presumably a meeting or two with some rebranding consultants, it became known as wheelchair rugby.

Wheelchair rugby was previously known as murderball, owing to the rather violent collisions between chair, floor and human flesh and bone that it encouraged.

Wheelchair rugby is much like William Webb Ellis's game. It involves picking up the ball, but rolling with it rather than running, and trying to carry it over your opponents' goal line. Men and women play in the same teams, and it involves quite a lot of contact as participants use their chairs and bodies to block and hold opponents. It became an official Paralympic sport in Sydney in 2000, and in Rio 2016 the gold medal was picked up by the Australians, who beat the United States by just one point in the final.

Players are just as passionate about their game as those of the non-wheeled variety. Mark Zupan, who captained the US Olympic team in Athens in 2004 and was part of the US side which picked up the gold medal in Beijing in 2008, put it like this:

> *Breaking my neck was the best thing that ever happened to me. I have an Olympic medal. I've been to so many countries I would never have been, met so many people I would never have met. I've done more in the chair...than a whole hell of a lot of people who aren't in chairs.*

SEVENS

This is the version of the game played in the summer on a full-sized pitch with, as the name suggests, just seven players on each side. It could easily be dismissed as an excuse for backs to run around and get their circulation going again, after a winter waiting out in the freezing cold for someone to pass them the ball. However, with a growing number of people prepared to fill some of the great rugby stadiums to watch the sport for hours on end, a little more attention is required.

Without lumbering forwards to get in the way, sevens is played at a much faster pace. As a result, the games are only played for two halves of seven minutes with a one-minute break. In order to make it worth the bother of turning up to watch, the sport's organisers normally put on a tournament with several sides competing together, and that is really where things start to get messy.

It is an unwritten law that when three or more teams are gathered together to play sevens rugby, approximately three times the combined weight of all the players must be consumed in the form of alcohol by players and spectators alike. Furthermore, to make it easier to remain with your team amid the alcoholic haze, it is more or less obligatory for all players and spectators to wear some kind of fancy dress.

Organisers of sevens festivals, such as the infamous Bournemouth Sevens in the south of England, then throw in a netball tournament, a few bands and a weekend of camping and, before you know it, you have quite an event on your hands. So if you are considering trying your hand at sevens, do take care and make sure you have a fully functioning liver before you go.

In spite of, or perhaps because of, Sevens' very boozy reputation, the summer version of the sport made its way into the 2016 Rio Olympics. Pass yourself off as a seasoned expert by noting that it was an English coach who had fallen out with the Twickenham hierarchy, Ben Ryan, who ended up steering the Fijian men's Sevens side to a Gold Medal and national celebrations and fame on the South Pacific Island.

BEACH RUGBY

Following the global success of beach volleyball, a few enterprising types have located a suitably flat seafront or commissioned lorryloads of sand to be dumped in the centre of a city and created a thoroughly entertaining new version of the sport.

Sand has the effect of slowing international backs down to the speed of the lardiest front-row player. This makes them appear to be slightly less challenging to tackle. However, forwards are normally reduced to the speed of a glacier and are, as a result, little more than useless in the game.

There are beach rugby tournaments played in places ranging from Majorca to Venice to Swansea; 2013 saw the first beach rugby tournament to be played in London, as 120 tonnes of sand were unloaded next to Covent Garden market. Corporate and club sides battled it out over two days while their friends, supporters and bemused tourists sipped their glasses of wine on the elegant balconies above the historic colonnades.

It is probably reasonable to assume, however, that, much as in beach volleyball, the main reason for watching beach rugby is aesthetic rather than athletic. If the social media comments after the London Beach Rugby tournament are anything to go by, it would appear that the sight of fit men running around on an artificial beach in skimpy shorts in the sunshine has something more than a purely sporting appeal for some of the spectators. The sun, sangria and the soaring temperatures seem to lead to significantly more pun-based team names. The women's teams in Majorca 2018 excelled themselves with names including No Women, No Try; Let's Get Rucked and of course, The Cunning Stunts.

THE BLUFFER'S ALL-TIME FIRST XV

You may, in due course, wish to turn your hand to bluffing your way around the professional rugby game – if not playing, then certainly watching and commenting. There will likely come the occasion when you will be required to have an opinion about some of the more established players and their approach to the game and, perhaps, life in general.

During any given season good players will come and go, and frankly it would require a great deal of effort to keep up to date with all of them. The trick for the bluffer is to pick one or two players in each position. That way, when you are stuck for something interesting to say about the bright young talent that is suddenly making an impact on the international scene, you can nod sagely, stroke your chin and, if there is a beard on it, clear out any surplus beer or savoury snacks that might be lurking, and reflect thus: 'Yes I suppose Tom/Dick/

Harry Speedipants may have a decent turn of foot but, for me, great players still need to have a bit of character about them, like...', and then pick from your pre-prepared selection of legends of the game.

Your choices don't necessarily need to be great technical players. They just need to have personalities and quirks, and fortunately in rugby there are plenty to choose from. Here, by way of a helpful set of suggestions, is an All-Time Bluffer's Invitational First XV. It is entirely subjective, reflecting the author's comprehensive lack of understanding about what makes a great rugby player but underlining his firm belief that to make the Bluffer's team you have to be, well, different.

TIGHTHEAD PROP

The Welsh international tighthead prop **Adam Jones** is the first name on the team sheet, simply because he has a fabulous mop of curly black hair that makes him easy to spot in the seething mass of players. London Mayor Boris Johnson christened Jones 'Cro-Magnon man', in a classic example of the sort of banter that one might generally expect between pots and kettles. Jones keeps his locks looking pristine by washing and conditioning them once a month, whether they need it or not.

LOOSEHEAD PROP

At loosehead prop, the bluffer might well be tempted to select **Jason Leonard,** with over 100 caps for England and the British and Irish Lions and known by his teammates as the 'Fun Bus'. Now providing great entertainment on the after-dinner speaking circuit, Leonard once observed in a conversation with Scottish commentator and ex-international Ian Robertson that, after a recent poor run of form, England would soon rise again from the ashes, 'just like a...pheasant'. When he was corrected he explained that he knew all along it was 'some posh bird that began with an F'.

HOOKER

At hooker, there is a good opportunity for the seasoned bluffer to opt for someone a little more obscure, hinting at a deep and detailed understanding of the international game. **Hika Reid** played in nine tests for New Zealand back in the 1980s. He scored two tries in his international career, which is actually not at all bad for a hooker. The first was where he started and finished a sequence that spanned the entire length of the pitch in a test match against Australia. His other try was scored against Wales, when commentator Bill McLaren was overjoyed to be able to deliver with some relish the line he had prepared earlier: 'It's a try from Hika the Hooker from Ngongotaha!'

SECOND ROW

In the second row, you can with confidence nominate another player who just happens to be easy to spot in a crowd, namely **Richie Gray.** That's because he is six foot, ten inches tall and kind enough to peroxide his shaggy hair. One of the few Scots deemed worthy of inclusion on the 2013 Lions tour to Australia, he can always consider a second career as a lighthouse when he finally hangs up his boots.

Next, you should fill up an imaginary pipe with imaginary tobacco, take out an imaginary lighter from your waistcoat pocket, spark up and inhale some imaginary fumes, and declare Irish pipe smoker **Willie John McBride** as your uncontested choice for the other lock. All you need to know about this man is that he invented the legendary '99' call on the Lions 1974 tour to South Africa. This was code for the simple four-word instruction: 'One in, all in.' During the matches, on hearing the call, or in the event of any altercation on the pitch, every Lion playing was required to punch the nearest Springbok. This gave the referee a choice of either red-carding the entire team or none of them. Oddly enough, no Lions players were sent off throughout the entire tour.

(On the first occasion the strategy was put into effect, there was a debate in the dressing room after the match as to whether Welsh fly-half Phil Bennett had fully entered into the spirit of things. McBride recalled: 'Someone said to Phil: "Where the hell were you?" Phil was reported to have replied, "I gave the ball boy a hell of a hiding."')

BACK ROW

You will actually want some talent in the back row of the scrum, and you won't be going far wrong if you select the All Black **Richie McCaw** who gets into most professional commentators' first XV. Dedicated to his craft, he told the *New Zealand Herald* that he had turned down an invitation to the wedding of Prince William and Kate Middleton in 2011 in order to focus on his preparations for the World Cup instead. That's the sort of commitment to the cause that makes the All Blacks the most successful team in sporting history.

Another Kiwi gets the call up for a place on the other side of the scrum, but for very different reasons; the late **Jerry Collins** played for the All Blacks 48 times and captained the side on three occasions, but it was his appearance for Barnstaple 2nd XV that gets him into our side. Having been spotted on his holiday in Devon in 2007 by the Barnstaple coach, Collins was invited to visit the club and help out with a spot of guest coaching. To everyone's surprise Collins duly turned up and the only payment he asked for in return was for a chance to play some rugby. Unable to play for Barnstaple's first team (rugby administrators do rather like first-team players to be registered in triplicate, several months in advance of every game) Collins turned out instead for the second fifteen against Newton Abbot. Back in New Zealand after retiring from the union game Collins bluffed his way into a rugby league fixture, playing under a pseudonym to dodge the regulators. Such consistent dedication earns him a place in our team.

And for a laugh you might consider selecting **Andy Powell** as your all-time greatest number eight. This is the Welsh gentleman who decided to celebrate a victory against Scotland in the Six Nations in 2010 with a trip along the M4 in a golf buggy in pursuit of 'munchies'.

SCRUM-HALF

You will, of course, need some backs, and you could quite reasonably offer the number nine jersey to Australian scrum-half **George Gregan.** Although now retired, he holds the record for the greatest number of caps for his country with 139 appearances in the Wallabies colours. He also has a claim for executing one of the greatest-ever televised tackles in a fixture against New Zealand in 1994. In the dying minutes of the game, as Australia were struggling to hang on to a 20–16 lead, All Black Jeff Wilson had made a 40-metre dash for the line. Having already seen off three defenders, he was in the air, diving to place the ball over the try line and apparently certain to score. Suddenly, a young Gregan, in his first international season, appeared out of nowhere and clattered into Wilson, knocking the ball from his hands and saving the game. Always useful to have a chap like that on your side.

FLY-HALF

Obviously you could have **Jonny Wilkinson** as your fly-half and that is fine. He did win the World Cup for England with a drop goal in the final minute of the final against Australia in 2003. However, you must bear in mind that with him he also brings along a lady called Doris, Buddha, and a cat belonging to the Austrian physicist, Erwin Schrödinger.* Doris is the imaginary woman sitting in the stands to whom Wilkinson visualises that he is kicking

*See *The Bluffer's Guide to the Quantum Universe.*

the ball. According to an interview in *The Times*, Buddhism and pondering on the quantum physics surrounding the life and death of Schrödinger's theoretical cat got young Wilkinson through a career wobble shortly after his 2003 World Cup triumph. Alternatively, you might decide that for the Bluffer's XV someone with a slightly more relaxed approach to the game might be in order. Someone like **Alex Goode** for example, who after a career that included 17 caps for England decided to retire in 2015, mostly because he really couldn't be doing with all the training expected of the professional athlete these days. After a few months doing little more strenuous than the occasional amble around a golf course, he received a call from Newcastle begging him to help them out with a spot of an injury crisis. Goode bluffed his way into securing a deal that involved him being chauffeured and flown to Newcastle and home again four times a week and squeezing his now not insubstantial midriff into the figure-hugging Newcastle number 10 shirt. After a few months he proved that there is still a place for the mildly unfit and somewhat oversized at the heart of the professional game and earned himself a place in our side too.

CENTRES

For centres you will want England's **Will Greenwood,** who is on some people's lists of 'overlooked-but-actually-quite-good' players, and makes it into this Bluffer's list for having the good sense to duck out of the way while the ball was being passed to full-back Mike Catt at the very end of the 2003 World Cup final. After being brought on in the extra-time period at the end of a gruelling final, Catt had one job left which was to kick the ball into touch to end the game. The only thing between the ball and Mike Catt at that point was an exhausted Greenwood, who after 100 gruelling minutes of intense rugby very sensibly opted to have a lie down at that point. The ball safely made its way to the superior kicker Catt, who promptly hoofed it into the stand. Not getting in the way is an important part of the bluffer's armoury and Greenwood gave a masterclass in the art form on that memorable occasion.

You might also want to give Irish legend **Brian O'Driscoll** a run-out, in spite of the fact that he was controversially and, as it turned out, correctly dropped for the last test of the 2013 Lions tour to Australia. At the time of writing he still holds the record for the most international tries by an Irishman (46 for Ireland and 1 for the Lions), as well as being the most-capped Irish player. Always a sign of a great player, O'Driscoll was singled out for a shocking spear tackle (*see* Glossary, page 116) in New Zealand in 2005 when two Kiwis, Tana Umaga and Keven Mealamu, picked him up and then tried to use him as a fracking drill for extracting shale gas. They made a bit of a mess of his shoulder in the process and he was out for the rest of the tour.

WINGS

The number 11 shirt goes to the late, great All Black **Jonah Lomu,** mostly for introducing the concept of the 'Maori sidestep' into the game. The traditional sidestep is where a player feigns to be heading off one way, only to then shoot off in the opposite direction, leaving the prospective tackler flailing around like a paralytic octopus. Lomu demonstrated his own version against Mike Catt in the 1995 World Cup semi-final. Instead of going round the England full-back he simply ran straight through him, scoring one of his four tries in the game. To aid the Bluffer's selection committee Jonah Lomu thoughtfully shaved the number 11 into his eyebrow to make sure he was given his preferred wing.

On the other wing, we might just lighten the atmosphere with one of the best Bluffers the international community of backs has had to offer. Australian **Nick Cummins**, also known as the Honey Badger has deftly turned a moderately successful rugby career, with 15 caps for the Wallabies, into an Internet celebrity status, thanks to his bizarre post-match interviews. His mop of curly blond hair and headband made him pretty recognisable to start with but his decision to adopt the fearless African honey badger as his rugby spirit animal takes him to another level. Describing himself as 'Sweating like a bag of cats at a greyhound meet' or 'Busier than a one-armed bricklayer in Baghdad' among other gems gets him on to our team sheet and doubling as the team's media spokesperson.

FULL-BACK

And finally, at full-back, you might like to suggest **Serge Blanco** who, born in Caracas with a Basque and Venezuelan heritage, found himself growing up in south-west France at a time when you could still be an international rugby player and somehow find time to smoke 40 Gauloises a day. After retiring from a career that included scoring 38 tries for France, he gave up smoking, launched a clothing brand and bought a few hotels before becoming head of the governing body for French club rugby and the president of his beloved Biarritz Olympique club side.

REPLACEMENTS

In the modern era there is plenty of room for a few more greats on your substitutes bench, ready to come on for the final 20 minutes if we need them. **Buck Shelford** the All Black who insisted on carrying on playing after having a ripped scrotum stitched back together during a game against the French, will be jogging up and down the touch line to keep warm. **Doddie Weir** with his tartan trews and general good humour will be bluffing his way around the inconvenience of motor neurone disease to come on in the second half and make a huge impact. **Martin Bayfield** will bring a little bit of wizardry to the squad, with his experience of being Hagrid's body double in the odd Harry Potter movie. And if things get really tricky we'll head straight back to the seventies and summon up Welsh legends, **Gareth Edwards**, **Barry John** and **J.P.R. Williams**. Bluffers will not need to know the details of all of their careers but a glimmer of recognition as their names are mentioned in the bar will suffice.

There's no point in pretending you know everything about rugby football – nobody does – but if you've got this far and you've absorbed at least a modicum of the information and advice contained within these pages, then you will almost certainly know more than 99% of the rest of the human race about what rugby is, who plays it, where they play it, and why. You will also know a fair bit about how to play it (probably more than most referees).

What you now do with this information is up to you, but here's a suggestion: be confident about your new-found knowledge, see how far it takes you, but above all have fun using it. You are now a bona fide expert in the art of bluffing about one of the world's oldest and most keenly fought team sports. And bear in mind that the only bluffing skill you really need to master is to talk a good game while avoiding anything that might actually involve playing it. That's never a good idea.

GLOSSARY

Advantage When a referee allows play to continue after an offence has been committed rather than award an immediate penalty. This is either because a) the side that has been offended against is getting along quite nicely, thank you, in spite of the alleged misdemeanour; or b) because the referee temporarily can't find his or her whistle. British author and sometime rugby writer Derek Robinson got it about right when he observed: 'The advantage law is the best law in rugby, because it lets you ignore all the others for the good of the game.'

Ankle-tap A desperate, dramatic, last-ditch attempt to stop an attacking player from running off towards your try line by hurling yourself towards them with your arm outstretched, catching a trailing foot with your hand and knocking them off balance.

Association Game How older, blazer-wearing, former rugby players refer to the game played with a round ball between teams of 11 overpaid and somewhat fragile little poppets.

Blindside When a scrum, ruck or maul is formed, chances are it will be nearer to one side of the pitch than the other. The narrower of the two sides is known as the blindside. If you are defending, this is a great place for the bluffer to lurk, as the odds are that you won't have to tackle anyone when the ball eventually emerges.

Blitz defence For the super-keen, athletic and well-drilled backs, this is the strategy of rushing forward as a flat, defensive line to intimidate the attacking opposition backs and panic them into dropping the ball.

Blood replacement A temporary player substitute who comes on for just long enough for your nose to stop bleeding, while you try and work out who it was who punched you.

Boat race Traditional and highly sophisticated post-match drinking challenge where two teams line up and proceed to drink pints in a relay race, signalling that each pint is finished by placing the upturned, empty glass on their heads. Things usually get quite messy from this point in the evening.

Box kick Scrum-half showing off by attempting to do the fly-half's job as well as his own and kicking the ball away from the base of the scrum.

Breakdown Not the emotional reaction to seeing your side beaten 68–0, but refers to one of various moments in the game where it is not entirely clear which side has the ball after someone has been tackled.

Charge-down Running towards a defender who is about to kick the ball away in the hope that they accidentally kick it straight at you, giving you or a teammate the chance to pick up the ball and score a wholly fortuitous try.

Conversion Not the decision to switch codes from rugby league to union or vice versa, but the opportunity to kick for goal and an extra couple of points after scoring a try.

Crash ball The hugely sophisticated tactic of giving the ball to the biggest player on your team and urging them to charge in a straight line through the opposition, flattening as many of them as possible before being stopped.

Deep Heat The fragrance of choice for all rugby players, a pungent lotion rubbed into your skin before a game that creates a strange warming and tingling sensation that temporarily stops you from thinking about all the aches and pains you still have in your body from last week's game.

Drift defence What backs claim to have been doing if they can't be bothered to run up at the attacking side in the slightly more energetic blitz defence. Apparently it channels the attacking side into running out of space or into touch.

Dummy The art of convincing a defender that you are about to pass the ball to someone else, creating a moment of indecision in their mind as they consider transferring their attention to the supposed recipient of the phantom pass, and thus opening up a small gap to run through.

Dump tackle The practice of picking someone up when you are tackling them and dumping them, unceremoniously, on to the ground. Illegal, unless you put them down very, very gently, lowering yourself on to the soft grass at the same time and saying sorry.

Dynamic stretches The way that sports scientists now think that you should stretch off your muscles before a game, by combining stretching and running around a bit while your front row watches, jeering from the touchline.

Feeding Nothing to do with bulking up on carbs before the game, but the term for when the scrum-half places the ball into the centre (supposedly) of the scrum. The word, however, is normally used when complaining that 'the little bugger is feeding the ball straight into the second row'.

Front five The collective name for the props, hooker and second-row forwards in a scrum and the ones who claim to be the only people who actually bother to push. Also known as the 'tight five', but usually in the context of post-match refreshment.

Gain line An imaginary line along the ground going horizontally across the pitch through the point where you think the ball might be during a scrum, maul or ruck. When the ball emerges, things are going well if you can get yourself and the ball over the gain line before being tackled again.

Garryowen The name given to a huge kick in the air designed to get the ball behind the opposition forwards, to give you and your team plenty of time to run up and get underneath where the ball is expected to land – where, with a bit of luck, the opposition's smaller and weaker players will be standing. Named after the Irish club that first came up with the strategy. Also known by legendary commentator, the late Eddie Waring, as an 'up and under'.

Grubber Name given to a kick through a defensive gap that bounces erratically along the ground and which the kicker will always claim was deliberate.

Hand off To use your hand to fend off someone who might be attempting to tackle you, while hanging on to the ball with your other hand or tucking it under your armpit. Slightly less effort than just running faster than your opponent and so is typically the preferred strategy of forwards. It must not be done with a clenched fist, unless the ref is unsighted.

High tackle Grabbing an opposition player round the neck in an attempt to stop them. Generally frowned upon and probably the quickest way of starting a fight on a rugby pitch.

Hospital pass A long, looping, lingering pass that eventually reaches you approximately three nanoseconds before an enormous opposition forward crunches into your side, breaking three of your ribs. You wake up in hospital.

Knock-on A politer way of saying 'You blithering, butterfingered idiot, you've dropped the f***ing ball.' Penalised by awarding a scrum where the opposition get to put the ball in and therefore will probably win possession. If you drop the ball and for some reason it goes backwards, that is still just as embarrassing but is not technically a knock-on so you can try and carry on playing.

Late tackle One made long after your victim has got rid of the ball. Ideally, though, it should happen on the pitch and not in the bar afterwards. Former Welsh rugby player Ray Gravell used to say: 'You've got to get your first tackle in early, even if it's late.'

Line-out calls The secret code used by forwards to indicate where in the line-out the ball will be thrown.

Rather dependent on having a hooker who can throw the ball a predictable distance. Needs to be complex enough so that the opposition can't decipher it but simple enough for your own forwards to understand.

Magic sponge A grubby sponge in a bucket of cold water kept on the touchline, thought to be able to cure all known ailments, from mild sprains to clinical depression.

Offload Managing to pass a ball to a nearby teammate while you are being hauled to the ground in a tackle.

Openside Not too surprisingly, this is the opposite of 'Blindside' (*see* above). In other words, it is the wider side of the pitch when there is a scrum or other interruption in open play. It is no place for a bluffer to be, especially if he or she is playing as a back, because there is a greater chance of having to do something useful – like running, kicking, passing or tackling.

Overlap When there are more of their attacking backs than there are your defenders left to tackle them.

Phases Not necessarily the midlife crisis that has brought you into the game, or teenage experimentation, but rather the moments of play, in between breakdowns, where you can actually see the ball.

Shoeing A method of gently inviting players on the ground to roll away from the ball by tickling them in the ribs with the studs of your boots and thus making the ball available for the scrum-half and for play to continue. For example:

Commentator: 'The Frenchman took a bit of a shoeing there, didn't he, Brian?'

Brian Moore (former England hooker, now columnist, commentator and all-round lovely chap): 'I don't care. He's a Frenchman.'

Spear tackle A dump tackle where your opponent doesn't put you down very nicely but instead attempts to insert you into the ground head first.

Touch judge A spare player from each side whose job is to run along the touchline and try and keep a poker face while lying about where the ball crossed the line.

Tunnel The little ritual at the end of the game where, if you're playing at home, you arrange yourselves in two lines facing each other and politely applaud the opposing team as they walk through the middle. This gives you a chance to count how many players and substitutes the opposition had as a way of trying to explain your embarrassing defeat.

Turnover When you go into a tackle with the ball but emerge blinking into the daylight several minutes later from under a heap of bodies to discover that the opposition backs have somehow got hold of the ball and look set to score a try.

Uncontested scrums An abomination where one team runs out of front-row players through injury or incompetence and, as a result, the forwards aren't allowed to push in the scrum in case someone gets hurt. Otherwise known as rugby league.

XV Latin for 15, being the number of players in a side in rugby union, just in case you had forgotten that this was a game invented in a British public school.

A BIT MORE BLUFFING...